# HOW TO HIRE TOP PERFORMING TALENT

# Avoid The 10 Biggest Hiring Mistakes

## AN ESSENTIAL TALENT MANAGEMENT TOOL

### Rob Andrews

*Creator of the Hugely Successful
LBA Hiring Management System*™

Published by

**www.lauder-beaumont.com**

Copyright © 2010 Lauder Beaumont Associates Ltd.

First published in Great Britain in 2010 by Lauder Beaumont Associates Ltd
Barn Studios, Gaterounds, Parkgate Road, Newdigate, Surrey RH5 5AJ
Tel: 0118 979 7798
info@lauder-beaumont.com
www.lauder-beaumont.com

Edited by Marie-Louise Cook of Clever Marketing Systems Ltd.
Design and layout by Clever Marketing Systems Ltd, Waterlooville, Hants.
Tel: 023 9226 1212
www.clevermarketingsystems.com

Printed and bound in Great Britain by
PPG Print Ltd. 18-21 Ordnance Court, Ackworth Road, Portsmouth, Hampshire PO3 5RZ
Tel: 023 9266 2232
www.ppgprint.co.uk

British Library Cataloguing in Publication Data.

ISBN 978-0-9565477-0-5

# Contents

---

**SPECIAL READER'S OFFER:**
**A FREE LBA 1½ hour consultation for 50 readers**
(see page 115 for details)

## INTRODUCTION

# The Pain of Not Hiring The Right Person

- Are you disappointed, even horrified by the person you've appointed? Have they failed dismally in the job?

- Are you sick of hiring candidates who promise the earth and then deliver mediocre results?

- Do you want to stop hiring the wrong people for the job?

- Would you like to introduce a system that ensures your hiring decisions are successful?

- Do you want to start hiring people who can deliver the results your company needs to keep (and expand) your market position and to become more profitable?

If so, you're not alone...

Hiring decisions are among the most difficult and important choices any employer ever makes particularly since the consequences of making the wrong choice can have devastating consequences for the company, its other employees, turnover, productivity, market perception and customers.

Yet, nearly two-thirds of Hiring Managers come to regret their interview-based hiring decisions, according to a survey conducted by global talent management company Development Dimensions International (DDI).

And it's easy to see why ...

According to a study by the global leadership training and research company Leadership IQ, 46% of newly-hired employees will fail within 18 months – that is, they'll be terminated, leave under pressure, or receive disciplinary action or significantly negative performance reviews. And only 19% will achieve unequivocal success. And that's based on the results of a three-year study by Leadership IQ of 5,247 Hiring Managers from 312 public, private, business and healthcare organisations.

It may well be a conservative estimate: nearly half of new executive hires resign or are fired within 18 months, according to the Corporate Leadership Council.

Research by Michael Watkins, former Harvard Business School Professor and best-selling business author, shows that failure rates for executive hires is even greater than Leadership IQ's estimates... he says 58% of the highest-priority hires, new executives hired from the outside, will fail in their new position within 18 months.

Whether the failure rate is 46%, 49% or 58% - it's obvious that something is very wrong somewhere in the hiring process. It is clearly broken.

And the effects of this broken process can be seen every day in small and large companies in every industry across the world.

Just recently, a publicly-listed UK company paid over £1 million severance pay to its CEO who'd been in the job for only eight months!

The company had trumpeted his appointment, announcing the new CEO would be paid an annual salary of £900,000 with the potential to earn three times that amount if long-term goals were met.

But eight months later, instead of reporting what he'd achieved in the job, the company announced the CEO's immediate departure.

What went wrong?

The same thing that happens in so many companies – big or small - somehow the wrong person was given the job and in this case, the mistake cost the company over £1 million in severance pay on top of the £500,000-£600,000 it had already paid the CEO.

It is a painful illustration of the financial cost of making bad hiring decisions.

My company, Lauder Beaumont Associates (LBA) has spent the past five years developing and perfecting a hiring process that works much more effectively than the traditional hiring methods.

We looked at the biggest mistakes Hiring Managers and head hunters make (we've included the 10 most common ones in this book) and then developed and refined a method that prevents those mistakes happening. And it's a system that your company, whatever its size, can use to improve your hiring process...

The *LBA Hiring Management System*™ has been used with our clients and the results are staggering... at least 86% of the people appointed using the *LBA Hiring Management System*™ are still in their jobs 18 months afterwards. That's a success rate of between 32 and 36% above average!

In other words, more than eight out of every 10 people that were appointed as a result of the *LBA Hiring Management System*™ are still in their jobs and doing exceptionally well. Compare that with traditional hiring systems where only four or five out of every 10 people are still in place after 18 months.

It's very impressive, I'm sure you'll agree! So what are we doing differently? What makes our hiring process so much more successful than other hiring systems?

The traditional hiring approach tends to be a hit and miss affair. It begins with a poorly conceived idea of the job requirements which then leads to a mediocre job specification. The search process is equally flawed: most executive searches identify and attract people with excellent CVs and impressive interview techniques – that is, people who are great at winning jobs but not necessarily great at doing them! Of course, this method occasionally hits the mark but that is more down to luck than judgment. Usually, the offer is mismanaged as is the induction and on-boarding process.

Our approach is very different. Unlike the majority of the hiring systems and methodologies, the *LBA Hiring Management System*™ encompasses the complete hiring process from start to finish – from the initial decision to hire someone to the onboarding stage – and because it eliminates many of the most common hiring mistakes, it's been proven to consistently improve hiring results.

It's based on 25 years of hiring experience working with some of the world's leading global companies.

It provides you, the Hiring Manager , with an easy-to-follow blueprint – so that as soon as you decide to make a new hire, you can use it to plot out your objectives, and then find the most appropriate high-achieving individual capable of achieving those objectives.

We're not saying it's easy... in fact, it involves a lot more thinking, planning and preparation than traditional methods but what we are saying is that the results are far more successful.

And surely that's what you and your company want...

So read on... you'll discover the 10 biggest hiring mistakes that companies make when they hire people but more importantly learn how you and your company can avoid them by using the *LBA Hiring Management System*™.

Put the *LBA Hiring Management System*™ into practice today and you'll be able to start finding and hiring Top Performers – the very best people who have the aptitudes and abilities to meet your company's current and future organisational needs and who will make a real difference to the bottom-line.

## CHAPTER 1

# The 10 Biggest Hiring Mistakes Companies Make

### 1. Lack of a Systematic Approach

Many organisations go into making hires without any real plan or system at all. They think "We've got to get someone to take the place of John" and call in the HR Manager to write a job specification.

Too many Hiring Managers are just left to their own devices. Without a systematic approach the new hire tends to lead to disaster. You might think this just happens in small companies who perhaps don't have the resources to create a department responsible for hiring but it doesn't. I know from working with very large organisations that it happens there too.

If you want to stop hiring the wrong people for the job, you must have an effective system in place that is followed every single time anyone within your company hires someone new.

### 2. Failing To Plan

With a very important decision like this in which you are investing money, time and effort and which will have a big impact on the business, you must treat it like you would a critical project.

The only reason for a company to hire anyone is for improved business results so the first step must be to clearly identify the business results you want and how you expect someone to achieve those results.

## 3. Unrealistic or Irrelevant Requirements

Hiring Managers often come up with long unrealistic 'shopping lists' of what qualifications and experience the new hire should have...

> *'The successful candidate must have a PhD in aeronautics, 30 years experience leading a FTSE 100 company, be tri-lingual and have the ability to speak in media-friendly sound-bites when necessary.'*

Sometimes they get so specific that perhaps only one person on the planet would be qualified for the role. And quite often, they are unrealistic about what they will have to pay to attract top talent.

Then there are irrelevant requirements. Hiring Managers will often have a list of criteria which has no real bearing on the job.

When you identify what the key objectives of the role will be, you can then work out what experience, skills and abilities someone would need to possess to be able to achieve them.

## 4. Ineffective Job Specification

Most job specifications are totally inappropriate for what is really required. They tend to be the minimum requirements for the role, in terms of skills, responsibilities, experience and qualifications, rather than the outcomes the new hire should achieve.

They're completely uninspiring and typically only succeed in attracting mediocre candidates.

For something that is so crucial in the hiring process, it's amazing how little time, effort and thought goes into the production of a job specification. Sometimes no job specification is produced at all and in many other cases, an old job specification is taken off the shelf, dusted down and updated to roughly reflect the requirements of the current open position.

It's no wonder that 99% of job descriptions are completely inadequate when it comes to attracting the best talent for a role.

An effective job specification should include a successful 12-month outcome for the job and the obstacles that would need to be overcome to reach them.

It should clarify what would represent outstanding performance. This will help to identify the small number of performance indicators that will determine an individual's success or failure.

It must specify the elements of the role which will determine success and look at the key challenges, problems and obstacles to be overcome to achieve them.

It's also very important the objectives and outcomes you specify are linked to company or departmental goals and objectives, otherwise they become meaningless achievements.

## 5. Ineffective Sourcing

For the majority of Hiring Managers, sourcing involves placing an ad on an internet job board, in a trade journal or newspaper and just getting basically whoever happens to come along.

It's highly unlikely that top performers will be attracted by advertisements in magazines, newspapers or internet job boards.

Most sourcing strategies limit the size of the pool that is fished in. Unfortunately, very few top performers swim in shallow waters, hungry for bait.

The majority of job advertisements are produced from uninspiring job specifications and are of no interest to the top performing talent that you are hoping to attract.

If you want to get top performers you have to be prepared to spread your net wide and to go into deeper waters. You have to know where they are most likely to be and go to them.

## 6. Being Seduced By A CV

Too much reliance is now placed on CVs –they're often regarded as the key data source for narrowing down applicants and even as the basis for hiring decisions - but as The Risk Advisory Group found, most CVs contain untrue information.

They're often filled with ambiguous statements and irrelevant information. They come in all shapes and sizes and are extremely variable in terms of content. For those reasons, it's easy to see why the over-reliance on CVs is a major contributor to hiring mistakes.

What's more, many top performers don't have CVs ready to go. They're happy in their current roles so have no reason to keep them updated. But not many Hiring Managers understand that: if a potential candidate doesn't provide a CV, he or she is dropped from the selection process. Many, many great candidates are passed over simply because they don't have a CV ready to go and don't have the time or inclination to produce one.

So forget CVs and start producing relevant and consistent candidate profiles in a format that will be useful when evaluating whether the person is a good match for the role and worth interviewing.

## 7. Making Snap Judgments And Basing Your Hiring Decision On First Impressions

Research consistently shows we actually take less than three seconds to evaluate a person based on their appearance, body language, demeanour, mannerisms and dress.

Unfortunately, these first impressions are extremely difficult to change or undo. Once you have an initial impression about another person you instinctively look for other clues as the relationship or interview progresses to support your initial judgement. This is often referred to as the 'Halo Effect'.

In a hiring context, it works like this: the interviewer decides for whatever reason that the person sitting in front of them is right for the job. They'll spend the rest of the interview looking for other positive qualities in the candidate that confirms their initial judgment (and pay less attention to the candidate's negative traits).

The reverse is true as well and this is sometimes known as the 'Devil Effect' whereby a person evaluates another as having less than desirable qualities and therefore looks for reasons to confirm their negative opinion (and pay less attention to any of the other person's positive qualities).

Unfortunately, Hiring Managers will all too often use these first impressions to make a snap judgment about whether or not to hire a candidate, as evidenced by an international survey[1] conducted by global talent management company Development Dimensions International (DDI).

It found that 44% of the 1,910 Hiring Managers it interviewed based their hiring decisions on 'gut instincts'.

---

1 *Are You Failing The Interview?* a 2009 Development Dimensions International (DDI) Survey of Global Interviewing Practices and Perceptions by Scott Erker, Ph.D., and Kelli Buczynski.

People say, "I knew within the first five minutes I was going to hire him" just because that person happened to be 6' 3", dressed smartly, had a firm handshake and was very articulate during the interview.

The solution is to firstly acknowledge your first impressions of a candidate but don't allow them to influence your decision. When you have a robust interview process like we have in the *LBA Hiring Management System*™ which focuses on doing the job in the interview, it leaves no room for the snap judgements based on first impressions.

## 8. Ineffective Interview Techniques

The problem with almost all interviews is that they're based purely on question and answers and focused on past performance. They revolve around what the candidates have achieved (or claim they have achieved) rather than what they can do.

Or the questions are ridiculous and irrelevant such as "If you were an animal what would you be?" How does that actually help you evaluate whether the person in front of you can or cannot do the job?

Behavioural interviews look at how candidates reacted to a situation in the past as a way of predicting how they will behave in the future.

There's an over-reliance on assessment tools like psychometric tests. If you do use psychometric tests then you need to understand why you're using them. What are you looking for in the answers? What are you missing? What will the results tell you about that person's ability to do the job?

What none of these types of interviews do is give the candidate an opportunity to demonstrate that they can do the specific job that you have on offer – during the interview.

We identify the right people by having them do the job as far as possible in the interview. It's much more effective than an interview based on questions about their past behaviour or irrelevant subjects.

## 9. Making An Offer That People Find Easy To Refuse

Many companies take so long to deliver the written offer that the candidates get cold feet and back out or accept other job offers.

I've known companies who've lost the best people they could ever imagine for the roles because three months elapsed between the verbal offer at the final interview and the written offer being delivered in the mail - their potential superstars had been offered and accepted something else.

And if that happens to you ... you've wasted a ton of money, time and energy and you'll have nothing to show for it! Don't let that happen to you!

There's another problem with the offer process that if not addressed in the initial stages can result in disaster. I'm talking about the package that is offered to potential candidates. If you think that this is a mistake made by small companies, think again: large private and public companies make this mistake too.

Commercial TV broadcaster ITV, for example, lost a potential Chief Executive when talks with the Board's preferred candidate Tony Ball failed over his salary demands and his call for a say in who should get the Chairman's job. [2]

2. 'Headhunters failing to marry talent with Britain's top vacancies' by Miles Costello and Carl Mortished, The Times October 15, 2009

So even companies you'd expect to know better make major blunders when it comes to hiring processes. Even they can lose their preferred candidate at the very last moment because key issues were not addressed at the outset.

## 10. Starting Off on the Wrong Foot

The new hire arrives on the first day only to discover he or she doesn't have a desk. Someone forgot to put the order through. Or the new hire can't access any computer files – someone forgot to let the IT Department know when the new hire would be starting work.

Small things maybe but they give a terrible first impression to a new hire.

There are worse mistakes companies make that really damage the relationship from the outset... one is leaving the new hire to find his or her own way in the job. Michael Watkins, former Harvard Business School Professor and best-selling business author, discovered that in many companies the training for new executives is non-existent.

Managers are introduced to their staff and new plush office before being left to fend for themselves, he found. This 'sink or swim' attitude is ingrained in the culture of some companies, where dropping a manager in at the deep end when they arrive is perceived to be a good yardstick as to whether they can cope with the job.

This lack of training and communication in the first 90 days can spiral into a disaster for both the company and the individual. Within this period a manager will undoubtedly face a myriad of challenges that need to be tackled. This is a particularly hazardous period when alliances and first impressions are formed.

Another major blunder companies make is not communicating the outcomes they want the new hire to achieve. This is often because the company has never identified itself what those outcomes should be.

Planning will help you prevent any of these mistakes.

Don't wait for three or six months or the formal appraisal time before you discuss key objectives and progress towards achieving successful outcomes. Sit down with them on the first day, a month in and then at the three months, six months and nine months.

## CHAPTER 2

# At Last ... A Hiring System That Works

Most companies – even large ones - don't have a hiring system in place and yet expect to achieve consistent and successful results!

I'm working with one very large organisation at the moment and learnt that in the past even people within the same department had different approaches to hiring. There was no consistency between the ways managers hired people – they each did their own thing. Luckily they're working with me now and I've insisted they use my more successful process.

Quite often within large organisations the HR Department will have a hiring system but it never reaches beyond the walls of their office – no one in the company uses it.

The reason the HR-recommended process is ignored is because people don't believe in it. They've never measured its effectiveness and therefore have no faith in it. There's also no accountability for whether they use the process or not. Hiring Managers basically have the freedom to do what they want, however they like.

And then there are companies who have no process whatsoever. The people in charge of hiring make the assumption they know what they're doing because they've hired 'X' number of people in the past.

The result of this lack of process? Disastrous hiring decisions whose effects ripple out across the company in lost productivity, slump in sales, poor management, errors in judgment, and low morale...

It doesn't matter whether your company is large or small you need a process that anyone responsible for hiring uses each and every time any job needs to be filled.

Making an effective hiring decision is nothing to do with luck or a magic formula... it's about following the steps of the process each time you decide to hire someone. You need to complete each step of each phase to make sure you achieve consistent results and hire the best people for the jobs you want to fill.

The *LBA Hiring Management System*™ is a process that has been developed and refined over the past five years. We continue to refine it but right now it delivers a much higher than average success rate of 86%. As I mentioned in the Introduction, the average success rate is 54% so if you want to gain a 30% competitive advantage and make better hiring decisions, start using the *LBA Hiring Management System*™ immediately!

## CHAPTER 3

# Create A Successful Hiring Plan

Too many hiring processes start with someone (often someone other than the Hiring Manager) sitting down and writing a job specification that they intend to use to advertise a role internally or externally or both. If you want to make a successful hire this is not the place to start.

You need to think about important hires in the same way you think about critical projects. The only reason for a company to hire anyone is for improved business results so the first step must be to clearly identify the business results you want and how you expect someone to achieve them.

This effectively answers the question of 'why' you are hiring someone, provides context to your search, and breathes life into your hiring efforts. If you miss this step, nothing else you do will matter; your hiring efforts will be doomed from the start.

In the *LBA Hiring Management System*™, we produce a Hiring Initiation Document (HID) which prompts Hiring Managers for this key information. As well as documenting the critical business results you need, it provides background and context. It also enables you to document a business case or ROI for your new hire, the people you anticipate being involved in the hiring process and their roles, plus a high-level plan with details of tasks and timescales.

This forces you to plan rather than allowing the hiring process to be a random act. This process can map onto any hire you're about to do – of course, there will be differences in terms of the people you want to involve.

You need to decide, for example, how many interviews you are going to do. We suggest two but you may have a good reason for wanting to conduct three.

Setting out the process at this early stage also forces you to look at why you are hiring people. You should only be hiring someone new because you want to improve your results. If it's for any other reason then perhaps you shouldn't be hiring anyone.

These are the sorts of questions you need to address in your plan:

- What are the improved business results you expect to achieve?
- How are you going to go about the process?
- What will your sourcing approach be?
- Will you advertise?
- Will you use a head hunter?
- Are you going to just look internally?
- Are you going to use referrals to find someone?
- How long do you think this process will take? What time scales have you set?
- Who will be involved?

- Are you going to involve your team in the interview process?

- Will other departments be involved?

- Are you going to involve other managers?

- Are you going to involve peers?

We produce what we call the Hiring Initiation Document which outlines all this information. It provides the framework for the whole hiring process.

Hiring managers are often and understandably keen to get into the detail of the responsibilities of the role and the skills, attributes and experience they are looking for but too often other key influencing factors are forgotten or overlooked which can lead to serious problems down the line.

Here's an example of an LBA Hiring Initiation Document. (See pages 26 and 27)

[For your template of this crucial hiring document, please see Chapter 12.]

# LBA HIRING INITIATION DOCUMENT

| ROLE: | Sales Director | |
|---|---|---|
| **DEFINE IMPROVED BUSINESS RESULTS:** (WHY HIRE?) | 1. Sales Growth – Double Revenues in 24 months<br>   a. New Business Sales – Acquire 3 x new £1M accounts<br>   b. Existing Account Growth – 20% increase, year on year<br>   c. Channel Partner Programme – 4 Partners – to account for 25% of revenue within 2 years<br>2. Sales Margins – Improve sales margins by 10% within 2 years<br>3. Sales Operations - Improve sales forecasting accuracy (+ or – 5%) and pipeline management<br>4. Sale Management – Evaluate sales team performance and develop talent plan within 6 months<br>5. Sales Remuneration – Develop new sales incentive plan to support sales growth<br>6. Sales Collateral – New sales collateral required in support of new ICT service management proposition<br>7. Marketing – Provide sales input to Marketing in support of new ICT service management campaign, increase new lead generation by 30% | |
| **REMUNERATION:** (Basic/Bonus/Benefits) | £100k Basic<br>£200k OTE (100% achievement of target)<br>Car + Pension + Health Plan + Death in Service (value £25K) | |
| **ROI STATEMENT:** (First year) | Costs | |
| | Cost of Employment | £235K |
| | Direct Recruitment Costs | £60K |
| | Indirect Recruitment & On-boarding Cost | £105K |
| | Total Costs | £400k |
| | Profit | |
| | Additional Revenue | £20M |
| | Net Profit on Sales – 20% Net (existing margin) | £4M |
| | Net Margin improved to 22% | £4.4M |
| | First Year Target ROI | £4M |
| **SOURCING APPROACH:** | Method:<br>External Sourcing Partner: Y/N | Executive Search<br>Lauder Beaumont Associates |

| INTERVIEW APPROACH: | 1. 1st Validation Interview – Lauder Beaumont Associates<br>2. 2nd Interview (Doing the Job) – Candidate Presentation on key industry challenge – growing ICT service management revenues in a recessionary environment<br>3. 3rd Interview (Doing the Job) – Working Session on new business acquisition and developing a channel marketing programme<br>4. 4th Interview – Coffee with MD (not an evaluation but selling company vision to the candidate) | | |
|---|---|---|---|

| INTERVIEW TEAM/ ROLES | Role | Name | |
|---|---|---|---|
| | Hiring Manager: | Steve Jones | Lead 2 & 3 |
| | Managing Director: | Brian Smith | Lead 4 |
| | Marketing Director: | Sarah Howard | Team Contributor 2 |
| | Sales Manager: | Brian Bowles | Team Contributor 3 |
| | Finance Sector BDM | Helen Torrance | Team Contributor 3 |
| | Major Account Lead | Darren Thomas | Team Contributor 3 |

| TASKS/TIMESCALES | Task | Week Ending |
|---|---|---|
| | 1. Arrange Briefing Meeting with Lauder Beaumont Associates (LBA) | 22/01 |
| | 2. LBA Produce Job Specification | 29/01 |
| | 3. Job Specification Agreed | 29/01 |
| | 4. LBA Produce Sourcing Profile | 29/01 |
| | 5. Sourcing Profile Agreed | 29/01 |
| | 6. LBA Source Candidates | 19/02 |
| | 7. LBA Perform 1st Interviews | 12/03 |
| | 8. 2nd Interviews | 26/03 |
| | 9. 3rd Interviews | 05/04 |
| | 10. 4th Interview | 12/04 |
| | 11. Offer | 12/04 |
| | 12. Offer Management | TBC |
| | 13. Target Start Date | 04/06 |

| ROLE AUTHORISATION | Role | |
|---|---|---|
| | Hiring Manager:<br>Signature: | **Steve Jones** |
| | Talent Management Director:<br>Signature: | **Lucy Trap** |
| | Finance Director:<br>Signature: | **Henry Parry** |
| | Managing Director:<br>Signature: | **Brian Smith** |

## CHAPTER 4

# Make Your Requirements Realistic And Relevant

Hiring Managers will often have long lists of skills, attitudes, experience, and qualifications that their ideal candidate must possess.

These can be so specific that perhaps only one person on the planet is actually qualified for the role.

I've told clients "No-one will have all the things that you want" and they reply, "Okay, if they've only got 75% of those requirements then we'll look at them."

So I suggest instead that they remove the 25% of requirements that are non-essential and focus instead on the 75% that they actually need and want. What's more, the skills, attitudes, experience and qualifications they are looking for often have no real bearing on the job.

And to make matters even worse, after stipulating the many things that they want the ideal candidate to possess, they add insult to injury by being unrealistic about the remuneration.

This idea of having a big list of requirements is so ingrained that it is difficult for Hiring Managers to even consider changing their approach. So they continue to create a list of specific requirements that don't match the job and then use it as a measure for all applications. It's no wonder that the majority of new hires don't work out.

Begin with the end in mind. Look at the outcomes you want to achieve. What obstacles or challenges will make it really difficult to achieve those outcomes? What will the new hire need to do to overcome those obstacles or challenges?

Most Hiring Managers place the emphasis in the wrong area. Rather than being specific about the job outcomes, they focus on the individual. They will spell out the qualifications, years of experience required and behavioural traits rather than defining what success in the role looks like.

Later in this book I'll cover the best way to write job specifications which focus on the requirement of the role and not the individual. Only once a 'success outcome' focussed job specification is produced do we turn our attention to the individual and produce a sourcing profile.

People compile a list of requirements without really considering whether those qualities are essential for the role and the outcomes they want to achieve.

Sometimes after a hiring mistake has been made Hiring Managers decide the way to solve the problem is to make the description even more specific.

Or they'll look at someone within the organisation and decide they want someone who is exactly the same. Or that they want a clone of the last good person in the role.

They try to replicate something that is almost impossible to replicate. Just because the last guy had a First from Oxford doesn't mean that the next guy needs a First from Oxford to do the role really well (or even better).

Be exact about your requirements and the outcomes that you are looking for, but don't be too specific about the person who can fill the role at this stage.

It makes no sense to have a list of requirements which may not be relevant to the role.

I see so many advertisements like this:

*"The successful candidate must have 10 years experience working in a similar position."*

Advertisements like this are ridiculous: the length of time someone has spent doing a particular job is irrelevant – what really matters is how well they have performed in that role. What have they achieved during the past 10 years?

Just because a person has been in sales for 10 years doesn't mean that he or she is actually great at selling. It's better to have someone who has performed brilliantly for three years rather than someone who has delivered mediocre results for 10.

Is an MBA or a First Degree really necessary for the executive position you're looking to fill? Consider that executives who will fit the role are likely to be in their thirties or forties and will possess a great deal of experience. Do they really need a degree?

Look at how many examples there are of really successful people who have excelled in their jobs but had very few, if any, academic qualifications.

Will having a degree really tell you whether a particular person can do the job or not? Not necessarily.

Qualifications alone are no substitute for real experience and proven success.

So how does this work in practice?

Let's say you're looking for a Senior Project Executive to manage a key £100 million project.

Typically, I'm told that the right person must be a Prince 2 Practitioner (a project management accreditation). The problem is that being a Prince 2 Practitioner only means a person has passed an exam – but it doesn't mean that person has managed projects successfully.

I know many, many project managers who have been too busy delivering highly complex, multimillion pound projects to go and study in the classroom. To deliver those projects of course they had to follow a project methodology. They simply couldn't have delivered the project successfully otherwise. But only the experience gained delivering projects will allow the pragmatic application of the methodology that delivers consistent results.

If you put two project managers in front of me and one is a Prince 2 Practitioner who has delivered a couple of projects worth £100,000 and the other doesn't have a Project Manager qualification but has delivered five multimillion pound projects on time and within budget, I know who I'd choose to manage my project.

So do you really want to stipulate that candidates must be a Prince 2 Practitioner?

Let's take another example.

I've seen sales job specifications like this:

> *"The successful candidate must have excellent sales administration skills and ensure the sales reporting system is accurately updated on a weekly basis."*

Now I know many very successful salespeople and most (if not all) hate doing any kind of administration and are hopeless at keeping reporting systems updated. Why? Because they love selling and regard anything other than selling as a waste of time. Clever sales managers therefore hire someone else to take care of sales administration so that salespeople are free to do what they do best – sell.

So if the core objective of the role is to sell, administration is really not so relevant. It shouldn't determine who is given the job. Would you ever say, "He's a great salesman and I'm sure he'll break all our sales records and close more business than anyone we've ever employed but I'm not going to hire him because we could never get him to update the sales system on a weekly basis"? I hope not!

Think about what you are looking for and the outcomes you want to achieve.

Within the *LBA Hiring Management System*™ we produce an effective job specification by looking first at the key objectives of the role and what success would look like, and then the barriers that would have to be overcome to reach those outcomes.

That guides the active route to the people we are looking for. We want people who have overcome similar challenges.

We spend time working with our clients to develop profiles of the people we want who will have the capabilities the job requires.

These profiles raise questions such as:

- What sorts of things have the candidates done before?

- Where might they be working now?

- Is this a position that is going to attract them?

- Will it provide the challenge they need?

You might say "We must have someone who has successfully delivered £100 million projects in the past because they need to deliver £100 million projects in this role."

We say: Think carefully. Why would someone who is really successful at delivering £100 million projects leave where they are to come to you? Would your job present any more of a challenge to them? Probably not.

What challenge could you offer them?

What room for growth will they have with your job? Will they see the role as an exciting challenge or something dull and routine?

If you want someone who has been there and done that, perhaps you would be better to employ an interim contractor. Interim contractors are less interested in career development; they are selling their track record of passed achievements. You will usually pay a premium for their services but you are paying for peace of mind. If you do go down this route, validation of their claims of success and achievement is absolutely vital.

But if you want someone who is going to be excited about the career opportunity you are offering then you need to approach the job specification differently. You must realise that top talent needs to be stretched. Obviously they have to have the capabilities to succeed in the role but you must provide room for growth.

Rather than only considering people who have done something exactly the same in the past, look at people who can demonstrate that they have done something similar but on a smaller scale.

So in the case of your £100 million project, I'd suggest looking at the people who've successfully delivered £250,000 or £500,000 projects. Your job may present those people with the next logical step in their career path and the challenge they are looking for.

When you identify what the key objectives of the role will be, you can then work out what skills or ability someone would need to possess to be able to achieve them.

You need to be specific about the key outcomes and objectives that you want to achieve and then look at the small set of people that are probably going to be capable of achieving that. At the same time, don't make the field so narrow that only one person in the world would qualify.

## CHAPTER 5

# How To Write An Effective Job Specification

The problem with most job specifications is they are completely ineffective when it comes to identifying and attracting 'top-performing' talent.

The typical job specification usually lists some high level objectives, responsibilities, tasks to be performed, and skills and attributes required. What they actually do is outline the minimum requirements for the role, not what would constitute outstanding performance.

Compare the following job specifications... for the same job, believe it or not! The first is an example of a bland and ineffective job specification (and one that I hope you'll never use!)

## Sales Director IT Services

| | |
|---|---|
| **Location:** | London |
| Type: | Full-time |
| Experience: | Executive |
| Functions: | Business Development, Information Technology, Management, Consulting, Sales |
| Industries: | Information Technology and Services |
| Compensation: | £150,000 - £200,000 per Year |

### Job Description

Sales Director - IT Services & Software

NB: Applicants and enquiries will be treated in the strictest confidence.

### Context

This is an excellent opportunity for an experienced sales director to run and develop the sales function within a highly successful software and services organisation. There is significant scope for development as the business grows to fulfill its potential and the successful candidate can expect a comprehensive reward package including a six-figure basic salary plus incentive and opportunity to share in the success of the organisation as part of the senior management team.

### Role

The role is responsible for developing and managing the overall sales function within a successful ICT organisation.

Key aspects of the role include:

- Operate as part of the management team, setting out and implementing the strategy for growth and development
- Work closely with head of marketing and executive management

- Identify relevant business development opportunities across new and existing clients
- Motivate, shape, grow and lead the sales and account teams
- Devise and implement sales plan and strategy
- Develop key relationships with clients and partners at senior level

## Skills

Required Skills and Experience

- Proven track record in management and leadership of high level, seasoned sales teams in services environment.
- In depth knowledge of the ICT solutions and services market in UK a must.
- Excellent track record of sales achievement - directly and through team management.
- Expertise in budgeting, planning, forecasting and implementation.
- Top class organisational, communication and negotiation skills.
- Ability to energise, motivate and drive teams with a participatory management style.
- Comfortable operating at head of function level with full autonomy and responsibility for budget.
- Ability to work effectively with internal colleagues at all levels and external partners and clients.
- A strong set of business values and absolute integrity.

## Company Description

ICT multi-solution organisation - software, services & communications.

## Additional Information

- Local candidates only, no relocation.

And this is an LBA job specification... I urge you to use this as a template whenever you hire someone in the future!

## LBA JOB SPECIFICATION

| ROLE: | SALES DIRECTOR - IT SERVICES |
|---|---|

**Are you tired of competing with the rest when you could be the best? Do you feel you've got the capacity to drive sales in an organisation to extraordinary levels?**

Our company is expanding through a growing reputation for Information and Communications Technology (ICT) service innovation and significantly reducing the cost of ICT operations. We'll soon be positioned as the dominant supplier of ICT software, service and communications solutions within London and the South East.

We're developing a new service management platform which is lowering the cost of ICT service provision to unprecedented levels and radically exceeding the expectations of our clients in terms of service and costs.

You'll implement a new business development strategy, coach the executive team on client engagement, and build a sales team that is rewarded by success – both at an individual and team level. You'll implement tools to measure, change, and evolve our sales process.

Two years from now, we'll look back and you'll be a key hero who helped transform our business development and client engagement model, leading to doubling of contract order value.

### Size & Scope, Number of Reports, Budgetary Responsibility, Location

**Location**

- London
- Role based from our offices in the City
- Travel flexibility required

**Organisational Structure & Management**

- Role reports directly to the UK Managing Director
- 10 Direct Reports – 4 Sales Executives, 6 Strategic Account Managers
- Role Responsible for professional development of Sales Executives & Account Managers
- Key Interface: UK Marketing Director

**Revenue / Order Value Responsibility**

- 2010 New Business Order Value Target £10m
- 2010 Strategic Account Order Value Target £15m
- 2010 Strategic Account Revenue Contribution £45M

## SUCCESS PROFILE

**Outcome 1 – Within 12 months, secure 5 new business deals with an order value of > £2M**

- Within 3 months, identify the top 10 new business prospects that have the potential to close in 2010 with an order value of greater than £2M
- Within 4 months, produce and implement a detailed opportunity activity plan to drive 5 x £2M+ opportunities to close by the end of 2010
- Within 6 months, qualify out deals with an order potential of less than £1M , which do not satisfy strategic deal criteria

**Outcome 2 – Within 12 months, secure 5 deals from strategic accounts with an order value > £3M**

- Within 2 months, review strategic account plans to support 'big deal' strategy
- Within 3 months, review strategic account team pipeline and identify top 10 accounts with £3M+ deal potential
- Within 4 months, produce and implement a detailed account management plans to drive 5 x £3M+ opportunities to close by the end of 2010
- Within 9 months, devise an ICT innovation seminar programme and sign-up 50 key execs from strategic accounts

**Outcome 3 – Improve sales team and account management performance by 30% (measured by achievement of target) within 12 months**

- Within 2 months, perform a sales and account team assessment review for all team members and identify skill gaps
- Within 3 months, prepare training development plans for each sales team and account team members to address skills gaps
- Within 4 months, present recommendations for sales team and account managers to UK Managing Director – no action, train, replace
- Within 12 months, improve opportunity conversion ratio to 30% from 19% by introducing stricter opportunity qualification and improving bid response quality
- Devise & Implement a new sales incentive scheme to drive individual and team sales performance within 3 months

## Remuneration Package

Basic Salary £100k
Bonus £100k (based on sales target achievement)
Car Allowance £9k
Company Contributory Pension
Private Health Care

## LBA JOB SPECIFICATION – *Continuation Sheet (additional information)*

To write an effective job specification to attract top performers you have to know what success looks like.

Take a step back and imagine that you have someone working in the job and it's going like a dream.

What is it that gives you that warm glow?

Imagine that it's appraisal and bonus time and your employee has now been with you for 12 months.

- What is the benchmark for success?

  What criteria are you going to use to evaluate excellent, average or below par performance?

- What is going to make this person a top performer and how are they going to earn that high performance bonus reserved for the top 5% in the company?

Let's imagine you're a Sales Director for a company that sells a software product in a highly competitive market. Let's assume that most of the sales for your software product are controlled by the major IT service providers and your company recognises that it needs a channel sales strategy but this is a departure from its traditional direct route to market.

And so you decide to look for a top performing New Business Sales Manager with channel management experience.

The Sales Manager will have a team of five each carrying a target of £1 million for the coming year. In the past 12 months, only two of the five salespeople hit their target and total sales were £3.75 million.

Some of the statements typically contained in a job specification for this role look like this:

## Role Objective

1. The objective of the role is to lead and coordinate sales activities, to meet and exceed revenue growth targets by identifying, developing and winning profitable business through direct and indirect routes to market.

## Key Responsibilities

2. The role requires key input to the sales strategy and taking full responsibility for sales execution, developing and closing deals via partner and direct channels to market.

The Sales Manager will also be responsible for building and managing a top-performing sales team.

Key responsibilities include sales development, relationship management, product knowledge, achievement of revenue goals, sales management and reporting.

Now think ahead and imagine what your new Sales Manager has achieved. What does success look like to you? It could be...

- The £5 million target was exceeded and the sales team achieved £6 million in sales

- Four out of the five salespeople hit their targets this year. The fifth didn't agree with the Sales Manager's approach and left three months ago. A new salesperson has been recruited and is showing good promise

- Two of the five salespeople are now focussed on channel sales and 50% of the new business came through channel partners.

- Of the four IT service providers signed, two now use the company's software as standard as part of their solution implementations.

- The pipeline for next year looks extremely healthy with prospective sales estimated at £15 million.

  The target for the each quarter has been raised to £2 million.

- Marketing is now generating twice as many new direct leads as it was a year ago as a result of the Sales Manager investing time to articulate a much stronger and more compelling value proposition.

The list might go on but you are beginning to clarify what someone would need to achieve to be considered a top-performer.

Imagine now that the job specification read something like this:

### A Top Performing Sales Manager Required To:

- Increase total new business sales by 33% in the next 12 months. An increase of 60% will be considered outstanding performance.

- Transform the current sales team and increase the number of on-target performers by 20%.

  An increase of 50% of on-target performers will be considered outstanding performance.

- Define and implement a channel partner strategy to increase indirect revenue by 25%.

  An increase of 50% indirect revenue will be considered outstanding performance.

- Sign at least two new IT services providers as channel sales partners, one of which uses our software as an integral part of their solution in preference to our competitors' products.

  Signing four partners with two using our software as a preference will represent outstanding performance.

- Build a £10 million pipeline for 2011 and increase target to £1.5 million per quarter.

  A £15 million pipeline will constitute outstanding performance with a new £2 million per quarter revenue target

- Work with marketing to strengthen the value proposition with the aim of increasing sales leads by 50%.

  A 100% uplift will be considered outstanding performance.

The focus is now on what constitutes success in the role, rather than a collection of intangible objectives and requirements.

Typical job specifications tend to list tasks that need performing ('Submit accurate monthly forecast using Excel') or skills that are required, ('Must be an excellent communicator'). It's ludicrous. Almost anyone can be taught to fill in some numbers on a spreadsheet... And as far as 'must be an excellent communicator' is concerned, I don't believe anyone can reach a sales management position without excellent communication skills. So why put it in a job specification? I've often seen statements like this: 'Must have boardroom gravitas' which is very subjective and quite meaningless when included in a job specification.

It's no wonder really that most job specifications are actually completely ineffective. A typical job specification is very bland and says something like:

*"The successful candidate will have six years experience in selling to the public sector."*

What you need is something that is going to really appeal to the top drawer talent.

We suggest you look forward 12 months and get specific about what outstanding performance would look like and then create a job specification like this:

*"The successful candidate will have penetrated two central government accounts and generated £1.5 million worth of business within 12 months of assuming the role."*

You see how we've moved away from something very bland to something that is very, very specific and which represents high performance in that particular role?

By knowing what you want that person to achieve, you can then begin structuring the job specification.

You look at the obstacles in the way to achieving those objectives and the specific tasks the successful candidate will have to perform to overcome those objectives.

This kind of job specification is completely different from the normal job specification, which tends to be lists of things that people want.

It makes it very measurable too.

The outcomes must be S.M.A.R.T. – that is Specific, Measurable, Achievable, Realistic and Timed. You must be able to measure the person's performance in the job against the particular objectives and outcomes you're looking for.

Another factor which is absolutely key is that the outcomes that you have stipulated in the job specification must be related to the wider departmental and company goals. If an outcome that you have stipulated is divorced from or, worst still, at odds with a departmental or company goal then achieving the outcome is either meaningless or may even become a black mark against the person's performance.

For example, let's assume that we have a position for an operations director and one of the success outcomes for the role is to increase customer satisfaction scores. But at the company level, the key objective is about reducing cost, they would like to maintain customer satisfaction ratings if possible but this is secondary for the need to drive down costs. The company objective and the role objectives are now not aligned. OK, in ideal world you might look to improve customer satisfaction while reducing costs but this might not be realistic. The point is, the key objective for the company is not to improve customer satisfaction, the key high level goal is to reduce cost and this is what the success objective for the role should be focussed on. Improving customer satisfaction scores will not been seen as a meaningful achievement unless costs are reduced whereas a reduction in costs with a small reduction in customer satisfaction scores will be recognised as a successful outcome.

Once you've followed these steps, you will have a fantastic job specification that really spells out what you're looking to achieve performance-wise – and make it much easier to match the right kind of person to the job.

## CHAPTER 6

# How And Where To Find Top Performers

The majority of candidate sourcing approaches limit the size of the pool they're fishing in.

This is known as 'selection bias' - e.g. they just take a small proportion of candidates that happen to respond to an advert. We know that people who respond to adverts are people who are either out of work or perhaps slightly unhappy in their current role. And typically the top performers don't fall into those categories.

That's not to say there aren't some excellent people particularly in this economic climate that are unfortunately out of work and looking for new jobs. There are certainly more good performers between jobs now than there were 12 to 18 months ago. But still that's really a small minority of all the people that are capable of doing the particular role you want to fill.

Limiting your candidate pool  sabotages your chances of success and the implications are serious. Limiting your candidate pool may have a damaging impact on the business.

 The problem with advertising a  job on your website or on a job board or in a newspaper or industry journal is that by doing so you are limiting the search to whoever happens to see it and respond.

This just seems crazy to me: if people are your company's greatest asset, why would you limit the search to the small and not necessarily high performing minority that happen to see your advertisement?

If your company is only as good as the people you hire, why wouldn't you want to search and find the very best person for the job rather than take someone from a limited pool of people that happen to put their hands up?

Think for a moment about the very best workers in your company – the 10% or less that you would put in the 'excellent' bracket and who really make the difference to your company's bottom line. Now think what would happen to your company if everyone you hired from now on was going to be up there with the top 10% - would it make a difference? Of course it would! So why settle for whoever comes along when that person might not be the best one you can get or really want?

Perhaps you can get someone 'adequate' to do the job with other recruitment methods that introduce a 'selection bias' but you should be aware of the consequences of hiring that way.

It bears repeating: the people who are most likely to respond to your job adverts are those that are currently out of work or unhappy in their current role.

And as I've said, there may be some great candidates out there who are between jobs right now and who are unhappy in their current role – but what percentage of the people who could be a fit for your role do these people represent? Less than 5% I estimate and I'm being generous.

Be aware too that organisations that do take the time and energy to identify, hunt down, attract and hire the best talent will have a competitive advantage over you!

So to make sure you hire people out of the top drawer, you need to widen the search. Hiring the best you can means expanding the search – unless 'adequate' is good enough for your business!

Let's look at the five different groups of candidates you're likely to encounter. Obviously it is difficult to place all people into any one specific box or category but for the purpose of sourcing it helps.

## 1. The Active Job Hunter:

The Active Job Hunters are aggressively looking for another job and will often apply for multiple jobs at the same time. They may not be very selective in terms of the jobs they apply for. If they're out of out of work, they may spend all day looking at advertisements, applying for jobs online etc.

People in this category are most likely to reply to your job advertisement.

Top talent doesn't really behave in this way: they simply don't need to. In the very rare occasions that a top performer does become unemployed, perhaps through redundancy, they are much more considered in their approach. More often than not they quickly have several opportunities presented to them and their dilemma soon becomes which job to take rather than which job to apply for. You are unlikely to find top performing talent in this group.

## 2. The Passive Job Hunter:

People in the Passive Job Hunter group aren't actively applying for jobs but they are definitely looking for the next position. The difference between Active and Passive Job Hunters is Passive Job Hunters are not actually applying for jobs.

Passive Job Hunters tend to be reactive rather than proactive. They're currently working but they are very receptive to calls and approaches from recruitment agents and head hunters. They are very interested from the outset. They are pretty much responsive to any opportunity that fits their dimensions. As long as it is in the right kind of ballpark, they tend to go with it and say "Yeah I'd like to be considered for that job."

Passive Job Hunters always have a CV ready because they are waiting for people to approach them.

Unfortunately, it is unlikely you'll find your top performing talent within this group. If top performers are unhappy about their current situation they will take responsibility for resolving their issues. They don't update their CV and sit back and wait for the phone to ring.

## 3. The Selective Job Hunter:

This group is also reactive rather than proactive. The difference is that Selective Job Hunters don't respond to all of the telephone calls and opportunities they receive and they really are very choosy.

They certainly won't respond to amateur approaches. Anyone who bulldozes in or who hasn't taken the time to understand the company and key objectives of the role are likely to get short shrift from these people.

They will be qualifying hard - looking for reasons not to go forward. You will have to work hard to convince them to take an interest in the role you're offering.

They don't always have a CV ready to go.

A good percentage of the top talent can be found in this group. Be warned however that they probably won't return your call; you will have to do the running. They will need a lot of convincing.

## 4. The Blinkered Candidate:

The people in this group are completely passive and not considering moving jobs. They're happy in their current role and they certainly won't return the call of a head hunter. It's not that they're rude but simply that they are not interested in other jobs and so see no point in having conversations with head hunters.

Their immediate response if you do happen to talk to them will be, "I'm happy where I am, thanks."

With these people you get a really small window of opportunity. If you are lucky and do have the chance to speak, you need to instantly and completely capture their imagination.

This is where the value of a great job specification and sourcing profile comes in. If you have done it properly then the approach that you use to get to a blinkered candidate needs to be based on some of the compelling statements that you have put together from that job specification.

If your job specification is just a bland list of wants, believe me the Blinkered Candidate is just not going to turn his or her head in your direction. They won't be interested and nothing you do will shift them from that position.

There is a very good chance that even with carefully crafted, compelling statements that you won't shift them from their position of disinterest. But just occasionally you will capture the interest of one of this group. That is why the approach of researchers or head hunters is all important.

Be aware that people in this group rarely if ever have a CV ready to go... after all, they are not looking for jobs so why would they bother keeping their CVs updated? There's no point. If you ask a Blinkered Candidate to send you a CV you will probably lose them in that moment.

Realise too that a lot of top talent will be in the Blinkered Candidates group. This, along with the Selective Job Hunter group, is where you need to go fishing. It is not easy and it takes time to find these people but it is where you need to look.

You may have the impression that it's where most so-called executive search and head hunting organisations look for candidates but in reality very few do. It's highly unlikely that a head hunting organisation working on a contingency basis could afford to look for candidates among these groups - it would just be too expensive to go fishing in these depths without any guarantee of return with the investment and effort it takes.

The executive search organisations or head hunters that do actually search tend to do so only in the shallow waters, throwing up the people who are actively looking for the next opportunity. Again top performing talent is seldom proactively looking and almost never responds to a job ad because they simply don't need to.

We have already said that they don't respond to amateur approaches either and they will quite likely pass on most opportunities presented. Even when approached in a really professional and intelligent way they are still not going to respond positively very often but just a few might be stimulated if approached in the right way.

## 5. Off The Radar Candidates:

People in this group are completely uninterested and unapproachable for the simple reason that they are utterly content with their jobs and their lives and nothing will make them move. That is it, they are untouchable. Of course, there are top performers within this group but there is no point wasting any time trying to approach these candidates because they really don't want to move.

## The Solution

You have to search wide and deep, not just in the shallow waters where you'll mostly find the Job Hunters. You will have to go into companies to seek out the performers who will never respond to a job advertisement and who probably don't even think they want a new job. Their response to your opening gambit is going to be "I'm very happy where I am" or "Move jobs? I've never thought about it."

How do you overcome their apparent disinterest? You do like we do and plan this part of the process very carefully.

We create a profile of ideal candidates and then work out where those people might reside and then, using professional and methodical research, methods, we seek out the best.

We make the approach and see if we can bring them to the table. A lot of them will still say "No."

Planning is absolutely necessary so that you indentify and attract the best people.

We do delve into the deep waters to find the top performers and we are very careful about crafting the approach so it is most attractive to them. This really comes from understanding the job specification and being able to put it in terms that appeal to top talent.

There's nothing tricky or gimmicky about this approach and it's certainly not pushy. We're not overzealous because top performers don't appreciate that. You see all sorts of tricks in this field but we're not interested in that. Our approach is always honest, open, and to the point but delivered in such a way that gives the best chance of stimulating interest.

So if you want to reach top talent, you need to begin with a ' sourcing profile', as we call it at LBA.

Here's an example of an LBA Sourcing Profile. (See pages 56 and 57)

[Your LBA Sourcing Profile template is available from the LBA website ...see Chapter 12 for details].

# LBA SOURCING PROFILE

| ROLE: | Sales Director |
|---|---|
| **Achievements & Experience:** | 1. Sales Growth – Will have been successful at growing sales within the IT Services market. Will have delivered growth through new business. Growth through account development and/or channel Partner Programme useful. <br> 2. Sales Margins - Not essential to have achieved increased profitability through margin growth but previous experience useful <br> 3. Sales Operations – Will be able to articulate proven method for accurate sales forecasting and pipeline management <br> 4. Sales Management – Will have previously managed a sales team. Will be able to articulate management approach and how to evaluate performance. Specific experience dealing with under-achievement useful – motivate, train, refocus, exit – how to evaluate? <br> 5. Sales Remuneration – Not essential to have developed a sales incentive plan from scratch. Useful if they can articulate how to structure a sales incentive plan and how/why it delivers improved performance <br> 6. Marketing – Will explain the level of marketing support they believe is required to achieve growth |
| **Profile Scenarios:** | 1. An established Sales Director working for a competitor in the IT Services market whose imagination has been captured by the innovation and growth, in particular the new IT Service Management Proposition. May have worked on larger scale deals in the past and has probably been through a similar growth phase with existing organisation. Pace of growth and change may have slowed and the motivation to move will be a return to this exciting, vibrant growth phase. <br> 2. A Sales Manager probably working for a larger IT Services competitor who has hit a glass ceiling. Desire and capability to take-on the challenge of a Sales Director position but recognises that the only way to achieve this in the foreseeable future is to move. Will have managed similar sized sales force but as a manager rather than Director – perhaps heading up a market vertical or new business team. Motivation for the move will be the opportunity to progress to Sales Director position. <br> 3. A board member of an IT Services company, perhaps an MD or CEO who has a sales background. Perhaps does not enjoy all aspects of the wider role and seeks a move back to a Sales Director position – it's what they enjoy and do best. May not have been an outstanding success as CEO or MD. |

| Source Companies: | Company | Company |
|---|---|---|
| | 1. | 26. |
| | 2. | 27. |
| | 3. | 28. |
| | 4. | 29. |
| | 5. | 30. |
| | 6. | 31. |
| | 7. | 32. |
| | 8. | 33. |
| | 9. | 34. |
| | 10. | 35. |
| | 11. | 36. |
| | 12. | 37. |
| | 13. | 38. |
| | 14. | 39. |
| | 15. | 40. |
| | 16. | 41. |
| | 17. | 42. |
| | 18. | 43. |
| | 19. | 44. |
| | 20. | 45. |
| | 21. | 46. |
| | 22. | 47. |
| | 23. | 48. |
| | 24. | 49. |
| | 25. | 50. |
| **Top Performer Attraction Statements** | <ul><li>This company has a strong reputation for innovation and have developed a new IT Service Management Platform that reduced operational costs for clients and provides a compelling competitive edge over the competition</li><li>This company is entering a significant growth phase. Having grown steadily for 5 years, they are set to double revenues to £40M in the next 2 years</li><li>The CEO believes that the appointment of the 'right' Sales Director will be one of the single biggest factors in determining the success and achievement of that growth over the next 2 years</li><li>The Sales Director will have an allocated budget and authority to shape the entire sales function to achieve the sales objectives including organisational structure, resources, sales incentive plan, collateral, market approach etc.</li></ul> | |

Once you have crafted a compelling job description start looking at who might be able to achieve the objectives, where they might work now, what sort of challenges they may have overcome, and what accomplishments and successes they might have achieved.

Focus again on the outcomes that you're looking for and decide from there what achievements will give you confidence in that individual's ability to achieve them.

Remember that if you want to attract top talent there has to be potential for that individual to grow. Yes, you need a solid indication that they can achieve the objectives that you set out but if they have been there, done that, bought the T-shirt, got the coronation mug and all of those things, what is going encourage them to get on board?

Money, you might say. In my experience, top talent is never just interested in money. If they are I would recommend looking somewhere else because the person solely motivated by money will be off in a flash when the next highest bidder comes along.

For the majority of talented individuals, it is never just about money: they are motivated by challenge and personal growth as well as money. Don't get me wrong: the package has to be out of the top drawer or you just won't get off the starting blocks. You have to put an attractive package together. Occasionally, top talent will move for less money but not often.

It's a mistake to presume that because of the present economic climate you can get access to top talent at under the market rate. Yes, there are more people looking for jobs but they are probably not the top talent that you are looking for.

Don't allow any unrealistic wants to creep in when you're crafting your sourcing profile. Look at scenarios and come up with the absolute essentials and remove the irrelevant requirements.

For example, instead of insisting that your candidate has 10 years' experience selling widgets, think about how you can attract someone who's spent less time in the job but has achieved well above their sales targets.

I am far more interested in over-achievement than in 10 years' experience. Ten years experience doesn't tell me anything about how a candidate has performed. Three years of exceeding targets selling widgets is much better in terms of the tangible and measurable requirements that you might be looking for. It indicates that a person has performed well.

Think of scenarios about why people might be in their career and why this job would represent the next step up for them.

Paint a picture if you can. Actually, paint more than one. You might have one that says "This person has probably left university at 20 and steadily progressed up the career ladder and is probably in their first managerial position."

Creating these scenarios breathes life into the profile.

So think about the companies where this person might be. Competitors are an obvious one but think outside the box too. Consider different fields if you believe their experience would be relevant too.

Challenge all of the pre-requisites that people put in.

What do you consider 'must haves'?

What must your candidate have to overcome the most likely obstacles they'll face?

Once you have put this sourcing profile together, check it. Is it too narrow? If it's so narrow that only one person could ever realistically meet your criteria, you need to rethink your profile.

So now you have an effective job description, a sourcing strategy and a sourcing profile.

Remember: the job specification and sourcing profile are two separate documents.

- **The job specification** is about the key directives that you are looking to achieve: the measurable goals and the challenges to overcome and the key tasks involved and what success looks like.

- **The sourcing profile** is about the kind of people who will be ideal for the position: where they might be working at the moment, what they might have achieved, the things that you are looking for that might give a good indication that this person can do the job.

This is not a short process; don't let anyone tell you that it is. If you do a proper search you will need to make many telephone calls. There will be many occasions when you can't get hold of the people you want to speak with. Top talent rarely returns calls about a new role.

There are no short cuts; it is a labour-intensive process. Most executive search organisations or head hunters will fish in very shallow waters. Many tend to look at their existing contacts and the people who are on their databases and perhaps place an advertisement.

We believe that if you are paying top fees for a head hunter (who will charge you anywhere between 25-35% of the successful candidate's first year gross annual earnings) you deserve more than a cursory search on your behalf.

If you decide to employ the services of an executive search organisation or head hunter, check out what their approach is. Make sure they do proper in-depth searches to find the top talent. They must endeavour to look beyond what is easy and obvious.

They need to look at each search on its own merits and say "Right, where do we need to go hunting? We may have some contacts in there that can help us shorten the process but that is not the only place we should be going."

For example, when we begin our contact strategy, we start afresh – we don't know all of the names of people we're going to contact. Unlike many head hunting organisations, we don't purely rely on our database.

Instead, we compile a list of perhaps 40 or 50 companies to approach. Sometimes if the industry is small, the list may contain just 10 or 20 reputable organisations.

We look at trade organisations within the industry and industry conferences. We find out who the keynote and major speakers were at major industry conferences.

Our search, as you can tell, is comprehensive and in-depth.

So I suggest if you're going to use an executive search organisation or head hunter, ask them about their sourcing strategy. Don't accept anything less than an in-depth, comprehensive search. This is how you can determine if they are going to do the job properly or not.

Whether you conduct the search yourself or use an external search provider, know that it is going to take time but the result will be worth the time, energy and money you invest in it.

## CHAPTER 7

# How To Avoid Being Seduced By A CV

Using CVs as the basis of selecting candidates to interview is a huge mistake because most people are creative with the truth when creating their CVs.

Too much reliance is placed on CVs –they are often regarded as the key data source for narrowing down applicants and even as the basis for hiring decisions - but as The Risk Advisory Group found, most CVs contain untrue information – they estimate 65% of people lie on their CVs.

The over-reliance on CVs is a major contributor to hiring mistakes. They're often filled with ambiguous statements and irrelevant information.

What's more, the fact that they come in all shapes and sizes and are extremely variable in terms of content makes it very difficult to compare one CV against another

These days, candidates can get professional CV writers to help them create documents that are designed to appeal to employers. Again, that's not the basis for selecting people that you want to take further in a process.

Unfortunately, a lot of good candidates are passed over simply because they don't have a CV. I know executive search agencies and head hunters who won't put candidates without CVs forward but many top candidates probably won't have a CV ready to go anyway. Why would they? They're usually happy in their current job and not actively looking to move. Why would you have a CV ready to go if you're not looking for a job?

I don't insist on them. I tell my clients "We're not really interested in the CVs – they're too inconsistent. You are often comparing apples to bananas rather than apples to apples."

I know a head hunter who in his 20 years never submitted CVs to his clients. He doesn't even ask for them, and he doesn't get asked for them because he delivers a short-list of his candidates to the client with a summary report with each candidate and that's it.

Forget CVs or at least don't use them as a basis for narrowing down the field of candidates.

So if you don't use CVs, how do you choose suitable candidates to take forward in the process? Do what we do and profile candidates. It can be very simple and it removes much of the spin that tends to accompany CVs.

How do you prepare a candidate profile? Use the job specification and the sourcing profile that you created and look at a person's ability to do the job. Talk directly to the candidate using skilled questions and techniques to validate the information that is presented to you.

After all, you are not running a competition for who can write the best CV; you are looking for someone who can perform in the job.

You need to remove the gloss that often surrounds CVs and instead focus on people's achievements, their successes and understand whether there is a chance that they can repeat their successes for you in your role.

Start producing relevant candidate profiles in a format that will be useful when evaluating whether a person is a good match for the role and worth interviewing.

And we're not talking about creating huge reports: our candidate profiles run to a couple of pages at most and they focus on the salient points which make the candidate relevant for the role.

This is a logical progression from the job specification (with its measurable outcomes, objectives and goals) and the sourcing profile, (with the kind of people you're looking for). Now you put candidate profiles together, based on the two documents that you have already produced.

You should be able to cut to the chase in terms of the salient and relevant points.

However, candidate profiles are not produced by taking someone's six-page CV and reducing it to two pages because that would just be an abbreviated version of what may be inaccurate information.

No, they are produced by talking directly to the candidate using skilled questioning techniques that enable validation of the information so that it is presented clearly and concisely without all that gloss that is contained in a typical CV.

Here's an example of an LBA Candidate Profile. (See pages 66 and 67)

# LBA CANDIDATE PROFILE

| ROLE: | Sales Director |
|---|---|
| CANDIDATE: | **DUNCAN SMITH** |
| CURRENT EMPLOYER: | ITC Service Excellence Limited |
| CURRENT ROLE TITLE: | Divisional Sales Director |
| CURRENT PACKAGE: | £90k Base, £180 OTE + Car + Benefits |
| DESIRED PACKAGE: | £100k Base, £200k OTE + Car + Benefits |
| LOCATION: | Reading, Berkshire |
| EDUCATION: | Bachelor of Science; Mathematics; First Class Honours Loughborough University , 1985 |
| INDUSTRY QUALIFICATIONS/ TRAINING: | TAS, SPIN & Miller Heiman Trained |

## RECENT RELEVANT ROLES

- ITC Services Excellence Limited – Divisional Sales Director 2008-to date
- ITC Services Excellence Limited – Regional Sales Manager 2005-2008
- Solutions In IT Limited – Sales Manager 2002-2005
- Solutions In IT Limited – Sales Executive 1998-2002

## Key Career Information

- Sold primarily break-fix services 1998-2000
- Joined IT Managed Services Sales Team 2000
- Move to ITC Services Excellence selling managed services & outsourcing solutions
- Over Target Achievement – 1999,2001,2002,2004,2005,2006,2007,2008,2009
- Presidents Club – 2001,2002,2005,2009
- Commercial Sales – Strong in:- Financial Services and Travel & Transportation
- Big Deal Wins:- British Airways (£40M), Barclays (£35M), Royal Sun Alliance (£27M)

## Situation Overview

- Duncan was not considering a move as he has enjoyed another great year, despite recessionary pressures, achieving Presidents Club again in 2009
- This opportunity captured his imagination because it represents career progression to the position of company Sales Director – currently Divisional Sales Director.
- Although the size of company, deal & team is smaller than in his current position, he is excited by the prospect of growth and sees a big opportunity for an innovative managed services organisation in the current market place
- It reminds him of the journey he went through with Solutions in IT, which grew from £60M turnover when he started in 1998 to £450M turnover when he left in 2005.

## MATCH TO SOURCING PROFILE

1. Sales Growth – Will have been successful at growing sales within the IT Services market. Will have delivered growth through new business. Growth through account development and/or channel Partner Programme useful.

2. Sales Margins - Not essential to have achieved increased profitability through margin growth but previous experience useful

3. Sales Operations – Will be able to articulate proven method for accurate sales forecasting and pipeline management

4. Sales Management – Will have previously managed a sales team. Will be able to articulate management approach and how to evaluate performance. Specific experience dealing with under-achievement useful – motivate, train, refocus, exit – how to evaluate?

5. Sales Remuneration – Not essential to have developed a sales incentive plan from scratch. Useful if they can articulate how to structure a sales incentive plan and how/why it delivers improved performance

6. Marketing – Will explain the level of marketing support they believe is required to achieve growth

In current role is responsible for new business and account development. Stronger in new business than account management and has always sold direct so no experience of channel development. Excellent record of sales growth in current role ⬚ grew sales from £235M in 2007 to £280M (target £260M) in 2008 and £377M (target £350M) in 2009.

Although revenue growth has been strong, margins have been under-pressure. Net margins have actually dropped since 2007 (32%) to 2009 (27%). Accurate sales forecasting has always been an issue for Duncan's division, "...but we have been exceeding targets so no one was too worried...."

POTENTIAL RED FLAG

Duncan is a strong sales manager and has propelled many 'steady' sales performers to achieve Presidents club. His management approach is 'open door' and 'mobile on' – he always has time to work through a sales scenario or specific sales problem. He believes that it's a myth that sales people are born; "it's a skill that can be taught." The essential ingredients according to Duncan are intellect and drive.

Intellect to really understand a complex customer environment and needs and drive to jump out of bed very day and work the next deal.

Duncan has not developed a sales incentive plan from scratch but has provided key input in the past. Sales incentive plans are key, according to Duncan and he wouldn't join an organisation where the sales incentive plan doesn't drive the right behaviour. His view is that you get paid for every deal you do (no threshold before commission kicks in) and there must be no cap (otherwise there is no point going for the big deals that make the difference and deals get artificially delayed until commission is due).

Duncan doesn't speak highly of marketing. In his experience they "over spend and under deliver". He says that he has largely learnt to live without marketing support, getting his sales people to generate their own leads. He has attempted a number of times to get marketing reporting into him because he "would get better results on half the budget" but the company has always resisted.

POTENTIAL RED FLAG

Asking questions to elicit such key information is a skill that can be taught. It is something that we've taught our clients.

The key to producing a candidate profile is to get people to relax and talk openly about what they've done.

You need to get their well-rehearsed lines and stories out of the way first. Listen carefully and make notes for later. If they want to tell you some things about what they have done, let them. Actually, you won't be able to move on until they've done that anyway: they'll keep dragging the conversation back to it until you've allowed them the time to speak about their achievements. Be patient: you'll get your chance.

The intention is not about trying to trip people up or finding a real 'gotcha' on their CVs. That's definitely not the point. It is not about trickery and trip-ups; it is a way to really understand the person's achievements and accomplishments, successes and the part that they played.

You don't need to be sneaky and go around the back door for this but you do need to be skilled in the way that you ask the questions.

Once the person is relaxed you need to draw out the relevant information. Again, the intention is to make a reasonable assessment of whether this person could match the role and whether you want to take this person forward in the process.

When we do this on behalf of an LBA client, we produce half a dozen candidate profiles and then discuss the best two or three with the client.

What sort of probing questions do we ask?

If someone continually uses the word "we" when discussing their team's achievements, we seek to clarify what that person's role was within the team. Or if someone uses the word "I" when talking about their achievements, we dig deeper to determine exactly what they did.

Let's take the example of a salesperson who says he closed the biggest deal in his company's history - a £100 million deal with a leading bank.

A typical Hiring Manager will say, "That's really impressive! Did you lead the sale? Tell me more about it."

The salesperson will then wax lyrical about the sale in the terms that they probably have used on their CV. It will be the world's best story.

At LBA, we would say "That's a really impressive deal! It must have involved a lot of people, both on the client side and internally within your organisation which will have bought its own challenges. Tell us about those challenges."

The difference is subtle but our kind of question will elicit more useful information. We know that deals of that size and complexity are not done by one person but involve people from several different departments – finance, law and HR plus technical people. The salesperson who claims the ultimate credit may have merely processed the order or may indeed have orchestrated that whole deal or anywhere in between the two extremes. The salesperson might respond, "I dealt with mainly the IT manager" and it is perhaps not the answer we are looking for.

Or they might say, "My boss dealt with the internal politics and let me focus on getting the deal done." Again, that's probably not what we are looking for.

If they reach for the white board at this point and start drawing out the client organisation and all the key decision makers plus the key stakeholders within their own organisation then we are probably on the right track.

It is not supposed to be a magic question but it is the type of probing that is more likely to uncover the real role they played.

Your first question might not reveal the true story.

As long as you know what you are trying to achieve, and the information that you looking for then you can keep going until you get it. You might have to rephrase it or take a different angle.

I prefer to do these kinds of interviews in person but sometimes it's just not possible. For instance, I conducted an interview on the telephone with a candidate based in Germany last week because it just wasn't practical or feasible for either of us to do it in person.

By telephone, the session will take up to an hour to complete I always ask the candidate to set aside the time for the call.

You might not get all the details you need in one go and might have to arrange a further call. This is much better than continuing for more than hour - I don't believe these calls should ever last more than an hour I want candidates to be alert and energetic, not drained and tired when they answer my questions.

## CHAPTER 8

# Stop Making Hiring Decisions Based On First Impressions

There has been a huge amount of research done over the years on first impressions. What this research consistently shows is that we actually take less than three seconds to evaluate a person based on their appearance, body language, demeanour, mannerisms and dress.

It's something instinctive. Unfortunately, these first impressions are extremely difficult to change or undo. Once you have an initial impression about another person you instinctively look for other clues as the relationship progresses or, in this case, as the interview progresses to support your initial judgement. This is often referred to as the 'Halo Effect'.

In a hiring context, it works like this: the interviewer decides for whatever reason that the person sitting in front of them is right for the job. They'll spend the rest of the interview looking for other positive qualities in the candidate that confirms their initial judgment (and pay less attention to the candidate's negative traits).

The reverse is true as well and this is sometimes known as the 'Devil Effect' whereby a person evaluates another as having less than desirable qualities and therefore looks for reasons to confirm their negative opinion (and pay less attention to any of the other person's positive qualities).

It's a common hiring mistake but most people don't want to admit that they have basically made snap judgements based on their first impressions. People get a first impression and then look for evidence to support that first impression and ignore the stuff that doesn't support it. That may be okay in everyday life where the implications are nowhere near as drastic or radical as they can be when we are hiring people but the consequences of making hiring decisions based on snap judgments can be very serious.

This is backed up by a 2009 Development Dimensions International survey[3] of 1,910 Hiring Managers from across the world. Of those 1,910, 840 (44%) admitted they based their hiring decisions on 'instinct'.

The report's authors Scott Erker, Ph.D., and Kelli Buczynski said "Businesses tend to be careful decision makers when large sums of money are at stake. Major business decisions – such as whether to purchase that new accounting system, where to situate that new facility, or which advertising agency to choose – require extensive deliberation that can last months.

"Like these business decisions, hiring decisions can be worth millions to an organisation. DDI's research shows that top employees are two to three times more productive than average performers: bank tellers generate higher customer satisfaction ratings; line workers produce more with fewer defects; star sales reps close more contracts at higher margins.

"Over time, this performance gap quickly adds up to millions lost in unrealised revenue and increased costs."

Some Hiring Managers believe being able to make hiring decisions based on their 'gut instincts' is a positive trait and somehow proves they are great judges of character.

3 *Are You Failing The Interview?*, a 2009 Development Dimensions International (DDI)Survey of Global Interviewing Practices and Perceptions by Scott Erker, Ph.D., and Kelli Buczynski.

I have heard Hiring Managers boast, "I knew within two minutes of shaking their hand that I was going to offer them the job."

That there should be any kudos attached to making up your mind without doing proper evaluations is very strange. We are supposed to believe that it is a good thing that hiring decisions are made by people who have developed a sixth sense and can judge that someone can do a job purely based on those first impressions. I think it's mad but unfortunately, it has somehow become acceptable practice and seems to be tolerated.

I know however that this hasty decision-making would not be tolerated in other areas of the business.

Imagine this scenario: a manager is asked to review a company strategy document for his Board of Directors and tells them, "I could just tell by looking at the front cover of the report that the strategy is excellent. I didn't need to read the content: I have a gut feel for these things and I just knew from the way it was bound, from the graphics on the front page and the font size that this was going to be a winning strategy." He would be laughed out of the board meeting, and then probably sacked for incompetence! Yet for some bizarre reason, this kind of 'gut instinct' hiring response is allowed to continue.

Let's be clear – we all get first impressions of people. Unless you become an android overnight, your human instincts will cause you to form a first impression. There is no point fighting that; you can't help but form a first impression.

What you do need to do is be aware that you will form a first impression. You need to then stop yourself from looking for evidence to support that first impression and ignoring the evidence that doesn't.

If you are really aware of it, and know you are going to form a first impression about someone then you are going to be able to manage the situation. It's okay to think 'I like this person' and 'I like that handshake' or 'This person dresses smartly and seems very articulate'. Just be conscious that is your first impression.

Likewise if the candidate doesn't meet all of your standards, be aware of that impression too.

At this stage, the candidate hasn't proved whether they can do the job or not. You've simply formed a first impression based on the candidate's appearance, handshake, facial expression and the first words they utter.

You have to be aware of those first impressions so that you can manage them. To avoid making snap judgements and first impressions one tip that we recommend at LBA is that you jot down your first impressions.

Writing your first impressions down makes you aware of them and that helps prevent you from being influenced by them. When I meet someone I quickly jot down in my shorthand my first thoughts. I am immediately aware of those impressions and it helps me guard against being influenced by them.

The danger of first impressions is that they can lead you to make snap judgements like deciding in the first few minutes of the interview whether or not you'll offer the job to the candidate.

Involving multiple people in the interview process is another way to overcome the tendency to form instant impressions and then make snap judgments.

However you still need to be really vigilant that you don't all form the same first impression. The danger then is that the consensus clouds the judgment even more. When I involve multiple people in the process I try to get everyone to write down their first impressions because awareness is the key.

Listen carefully to what the candidate says, and don't look to trip up the people that don't strike a chord with you immediately. It's something I've seen happen so often – an interviewer decides during the first five minutes there's something they don't like about the candidate and spend the rest of the interview trying to trip them up.

And I've seen interviewers help the candidates that they like and make it easy for them.

Be measured and try and extend the same courtesy towards all the candidates - you want them to feel relaxed and do the best they can. Very often the bad first impressions are created because the candidate is a little nervous. People do get nervous, even top performers, so don't be officious. Allow them to warm up and give them a chance.

When you have a robust interview process like we have in the *LBA Hiring Management System*™ which focuses on doing the job in the interview, it leaves no room for the snap judgements based on first impressions.

If you decide from the outset that you are going to use a two-step interview process and that the first will be a validating interview and the second will involve the candidate doing the job there will be no point making a snap judgement. You will know you have a process to follow, and there is no need to make a snap judgement during or after the first interview.

The validation interview is to confirm what candidates have said in the conversations that you have had with them thus far or what they have claimed in their CV.

Really good candidates may want to help you tackle a real problem or goal in the very first interview, because that is good practice and good technique. You are allowed to feel good about the fact that your candidate wants to take control and wants to show you what they can do and it's usually a really good sign that you have got an excellent candidate in front of you. But you need to explain that they will have the opportunity to show that they can solve problems and meet the specific challenges that you've got in the second interview.

When you follow the right process it will be quite obvious that you have found an excellent top performing candidate.

In the *LBA Hiring Management System*™, we encourage you to define your hiring processes at the start. You may decide that you need two, three or four interviews, which is fine provided that you define the purpose of those meetings and that one of those interviews will be a working session.

## CHAPTER 9

# How To Conduct Effective Interviews

The majority (a whopping 66%) of Hiring Managers regret their interview-based hiring decisions, according to the DDI.

The fact that two-thirds of those decisions are cause for regret is alarming, I think you would agree. Certainly, it shows that something is very wrong with the current interview process.

Actually, I think it is quite a staggering statistic particularly when you consider this is an area where vast sums of money is invested by organisations in the hope of improving interview techniques.

You would think with all the investment in programmes that profess to teach superior interview techniques that Hiring Managers would get better at it but unfortunately they are being trained in ineffective flawed techniques. It's not surprising that they don't get better results.

Some bigger companies are very prescriptive about the interview content and process and ensure that every candidate is asked the same set of questions and the Hiring Managers diligently look at the answers and records and scrutinises them afterwards and make judgments based on them. But generally, most companies have no structure.

I've found that more often than not Hiring Managers within the same department use different approaches.

In fact, I think people would be really surprised how much variation there is within a department, let alone a company. It is quite amazing to me that hiring is so often left to individual preference. Some people just hire who they like personally.

And some interviewers like to think they are tough and like to put candidates under pressure and ask them the most difficult interview questions and let them squirm. I know that only a desperate job hunter would put up with this interrogation style interview. You can't treat top performers in that way. They'll walk out and you'll never see them again. You can put them under pressure to come up with how they would achieve the real objective that you are looking for in the job. That is acceptable pressure. Firing questions at them to make them squirm is unacceptable pressure and it's also ineffective.

The problem with all interviews is that they are purely question and answer-based and focused on past performance. They're all about what candidates have done, or claim they have done, rather than what they can do.

There are many different types of interviews: telephone, face to face and one to one, panel based, computer based, it goes on and on.

One of the most popular types of interview is the competence or behavioural-based interview which assess past performances as an indicator of possible future performance. An example would be to ask the candidate to describe a situation in which they were able to use persuasion to successfully convince someone to see things their way.

When someone finishes answering a question about their previous experience I don't think I'm any further forward in understanding whether they can do my job or not.

If you have key things that you want the new hire to perform and achieve in the job, isn't it better to focus on one of them rather than ask an abstract question about something in the past?

Chronological-type interviews are also very popular. The Hiring Manager will ask candidates to talk about their career from the start through to the present day.

The interviewer will say, "Talk me through your CV."

The candidate might be asked to explain why they made certain choices or why their background and experience make them a suitable candidate for the job.

It's a little bit less structured than the competency-based interview but the interviewer is trying to find the reasons behind career and life decisions and get the candidate to elaborate on points of interest.

The problem with both of these types of interviews is that they are all historic and a well-prepared candidate will know what is coming and can prepare for the answers.

There is an entire industry that helps people prepare for interviews like these. Candidates can go to websites and be grilled by 'mock' interviewers. They can find out the toughest, trickiest (puzzle) interview questions and prepare their answers.

Candidates know that if they deliver certain responses they're more likely to get the job.

We don't want candidates to demonstrate their knowledge of 'winning' interview techniques – we're only interested in those that can show us they are capable of doing the job.

Most interviews don't give candidates the opportunity to prove that they can do the specific job that you have on offer there and then in the interview. I think they should and I think it can be done.

That's why the *LBA Hiring Management System*™ provides a framework for guidance for designing an interview to get the candidate either doing the job or at least parts of the job in the interview and really tackling problems that they will be responsible for should they secure the role.

That means you, as Hiring Manager, uses the meeting as a working session with a colleague rather than a traditional question-and-answer type interview, which statistics prove don't produce the best results.

You can invite other team members and colleagues to join in the working session, which provides an opportunity to assess how candidates interact and work with the team.

It might stretch over more than one session but that's okay.

With the LBA approach there are no clever or perfect answers to questions but doing the job leaves candidates nowhere to hide.

In fact, high performers aren't looking for hiding places – they're looking for opportunities to shine. They can't wait to show you what they can do. They are talented individuals who want to demonstrate their capability.

This is how you are going to make better hiring decisions and it can be done.

Let's say you're looking for a Sales Manager. You've prepared a fantastic LBA job specification and have the key objectives that will produce success in the role.

How can you structure an interview to look at one of those outcomes? How could they work through the known challenges or obstacles to achieve that objective?

Alright, your candidates won't necessarily have all the information at hand to get it absolutely nailed but it is going to be close. What's more, you will see how they approach the challenge.

Use real challenges and let them be the focus of the interview.

For example, if one of the key objectives is to get an additional £1 million in sales from the financial services market by gaining two new clients within 12 months, then you'd use the working session to explore how the candidate would penetrate that market and get two new clients.

Don't allow the session to become just questions and answers - get them to do a presentation about it and work through it.

Equally, don't let this be a one-way thing where your candidate does all the hard graft: you have got to roll your sleeves up and treat it like a working meeting. Pull others into the meeting.

The real test, the real proof, comes down to whether they can actually do the job.

If you were hiring a telesales person who was going to have to make cold calls to companies and sell advertising space all day, what better way to judge whether that person can do the job or not than set up a simulation? Tell the candidates in advance what you're going to do and then set up the situation, using fake or real clients. You can have some preliminary introduction where you explain the role and the objectives you want them to reach. And then let them show you how they'd sell advertising space over the phone.

The crux of the matter is that you're going to listen to them make some cold calls. You'll hear how they perform doing the job you want them to do.

If you're hiring an expert I can't think of a better or more sensible way to evaluate their suitability for the position than getting them to do it there and then.

Of course, you'll have other considerations that you want to measure but surely the number one is: can this person perform the job that you need doing?

Most people hiring at executive level say, "Look, the breadth of this role is so big, and there are lots of different areas of responsibility, you can't possibly replicate that and get candidates to address them in one, two, or three hours of interviews!"

My answer is: I believe you can simulate a lot of that within the process. If there are too many areas to tackle, take one or two and maybe work that through.

Let's take an example then for an executive hire. Let's say this person is going to be a new Financial Services Sales Manager for an IT company.

The successful candidate will have to develop new business within a financial services sector where the company has a limited track record with two or three clients. It needs to get six or seven more new clients.

The company has had a bit of success in the financial services sector but has struggled to expand further. It hasn't penetrated the market in the way it wants or needs to, hence the decision to hire a new Financial Services Sales Manager.

As Hiring Manager, you would say, "This is the problem. This is the product or service that we have. We know that it's technically superior to our competitors' products but most of them have been in this market longer and have more established reputations. The price of our product is competitive but the set-up costs are higher and it takes a little longer to implement. How would you go about penetrating that marketplace? Let's make it a whiteboard session... Let's work on the specific problem that we have."

What happens next will be far more revealing in terms of whether the candidate can perform in the role than saying, "Tell me about your previous experience. How did you break into the financial service sector?" That's historic; it's with a different company and a different set of products or services and different challenges.

And just because they've done it in the past, it doesn't prove they can do it for your company.

You can't absolutely prove the candidate will be able to perform but you can simulate the real job and its challenges as much as possible.

The candidate won't get it 100% right but you will be able to see the way they approach it and whether they're systematic, methodical, innovative or entrepreneurial in their approach.

This will help you determine if they can meet your specific challenges. No two companies, no two jobs are exactly the same even if they have the same title within the same sector, they will be different. There are no two identical companies out there.

You need to have the confidence that the person you eventually hire can do the job in your company the way you want it done with a profitable outcome.

You also need to know they can work with your existing team so make sure that you include them in the process; if that means arranging a second meeting, so be it.

Get them involved and watch how they work with other people in the company. Are they a good fit for the culture?

Some evaluation centres encourage this kind of interview but tend not to prepare candidates beforehand... they don't let them know exactly what is going to happen so it's a bit of a surprise.

I believe this is wrong: you wouldn't ask anyone to do a job without any preparation so why not give candidates advance warning so that they can prepare and perform at their very best on the day?

There's an idea that springing an interview like this on candidates is ideal for simulating on-the-job pressure. Some Hiring Managers want to see how candidates will cope with pressure. I don't agree with this: being completely unprepared and caught on the hop is just stressful and that's not the same kind of pressure as they'll experience on-the-job.

Why not do what we do at LBA and actually ask candidates to achieve one of the objectives of the real job? That's a real pressure that they are going to face when they are doing the job, not some kind of phoney pressure created as a result of being caught on the hop.

Simulating the job could take place over one, a couple or even a series of sessions.

In the first of those sessions you might want to pick a problem that is generic to the industry.

Let's say your company is involved in selling IT services to the public sector. Perhaps budgets have been slashed in the public sector and that is causing everyone a problem. You could ask your candidate how that problem could be tackled. If that session goes well, the second might look at the specific problems to be solved in your company. You'd refer back to your job specification which outlines those and makes them very clear.

Some general points: Make sure that you stipulate your interview process up front. Use the hiring initiation document to outline your process. Make sure everyone involved understands it and that the process is planned. Everyone must know what you're trying to achieve and why.

Plan the number of meetings you'll have and what each one means. So what is meeting number two going to be about and what will it mean in terms of making a choice about candidates? Will it be a rubber stamp? Will further evaluation be necessary? How will it help you to reach the final decision?

And then there are the more obvious things that must be planned like devoting the right kind of time to each session, and making sure the interviews are held in the right environment – one that it is pleasant and welcoming.

And we don't make the post-interview evaluation a vastly complicated affair. We believe it should be as simple as the Hiring Manager and whoever else is involved in the decision process meeting in person or by telephone. The Hiring Manager then speaks very clearly about the person they believe is the ideal candidate and how they performed in the interview. If the process we recommend has been followed, the choice of ideal candidate should be glaringly obvious.

If the Hiring Manager can't decide which of the three or four top candidates would the ideal person for the job, they need to go back through the process again because they haven't seen the right people.

In summary, the LBA interview approach is all about placing less reliance on the candidate's history and more about their ability to do the job you want in the present. It's about allowing the candidates to work at achieving the goals and objectives of the job, and overcoming obstacles.

This is what enables LBA to get more reliable results more often from interviews. It also helps Hiring Managers to make better decisions. For as I've shown, Hiring Managers who use the traditional ineffective hiring methods come to regret the decisions they make 66% of the time.

## CHAPTER 10

# How To Make An Offer People Can't Refuse

The offer management process is something that companies and in particular Hiring Managers need to take more seriously.

Typically, the Hiring Manager gives a huge sigh of relief after the candidate accepts a verbal job offer and thinks, "Great, we found an excellent person for for the job – that's another problem taken care of. Now I can get on with my day job."

Unfortunately, it's not as simple as that and in fact that's where a lot of things fall down.

First there is a way of handling the offer itself that makes a successful outcome for both parties more likely.

Having identified the person that you want to hire, the next step naturally is to negotiate and hopefully reach agreement about an offer. It is unlikely that there will be no negotiation at all.

The important thing is that the parameters of the offer are discussed very early in the process. When we are involved, we discuss the remuneration during the initial conversation we have with the candidate.

There should be no big surprises once you get to the offer part of the process. It should be a matter of a few little things here and there in negotiation. It certainly shouldn't be an overly drawn out part of the process.

It's wise to expect some negotiation to take place and as the Hiring Manager you need to leave some room to manoeuvre within that. Some organisations have strict guidelines about the terms of engagement but most companies have some flexibility built in.

If the deal falls through at this stage then it is because expectations weren't set effectively in the introductory phase.

If you are using the services of a head hunter, allow them to negotiate the offer on your behalf. It is their job to be the intermediary and makes it easier for both parties. The candidate is likely to be more open about his or her expectations with a third party.

Don't allow the process to drag out. Remember, time kills deals. If you meet with an individual who is ideal for the role that you want to hire tomorrow, why wait?

Hiring managers will say things like, "You are definitely on my short list but I'm seeing six candidates over the next six weeks..." By the time the second interview takes place, weeks have gone by and the ideal candidate may have been offered a new role by their existing employer, or been snatched up by a nimbler organisation.

The way to avoid this is to not allow the interview process to be too long or drawn out. If you really are interviewing six candidates then conduct those interviews in one week.

When you find your ideal candidate, make it clear to them that you want them on board. That will change everything for them. Suddenly, the new role with an existing employer won't look so attractive and they are more likely to turn down the advances of other head hunters.

High performing talent knows when the interview process has gone well and the job is ideal for them. Often, they're ready to accept an offer on the spot should you make one. But they can easily become disillusioned if you don't share their enthusiasm.

Candidates report back comments like, "I love what I heard at the interview but to be honest I don't want to work for an organisation that takes six weeks to make a decision."

If you find your ideal candidate, move quickly to secure their services. Once your ideal candidate has accepted your verbal offer, the written agreement and contract must follow as soon as possible.

Naturally people want to see the agreement in black and white particularly before they hand in their notice to a current employer.

Unfortunately, this is where the whole process can go awry, particularly in large organisations where the whole hiring process is very slow and the HR Department has a backlog of contracts to deal with.

As Hiring Manger, you can't afford to shrug your shoulders and accept the delay. If you want that candidate on board you need to ride that process hard. Make sure your offer doesn't slowly make its way to the top of the pile or get lost somewhere between the HR Manager's desk and the person who signs it off.

There is nothing worse for a candidate than receiving a verbal offer and then waiting for three weeks or more for someone to come through with the paperwork.

The delay reflects badly on you, the Hiring Manager, irrespective of whether it is HR's responsibility or not.

One candidate told me, "I was really impressed with the Hiring Manager and I really thought that he was someone I wanted to work for, but if he doesn't have the influence to make people get the offer to me in a timely fashion then I'm just not sure.

"I know it's not his fault but if the company is really so bureaucratic that it takes three weeks to get something out of the door then I'm not sure that is an organisation I want to work for."

You owe it to yourself and the candidate you want to get on board to understand exactly what the offer process is and who is involved.

In fact, the sign off process should be identified at the outset (and is Phase 1 of the *LBA Hiring Management System*™). That way, you'll know what that process is and who has got to sign off.

If you're getting towards the final interview stage and you know that you'll be making an offer, pick up the phone and say "This is really important to me: I've got this new hire coming on board and I just want to make sure you are going to be around next week to get this signed off."

Talk to people directly. When I was hiring people, and the current turnaround time for written offers was two weeks I used to telephone whoever was responsible for processing offers and say, "What can we really do to sort this out in a week? What can I do to help make that happen?"

If the offer needs to go through an authorisation process then find out who needs to sign it off and pick up the phone and tell them everything they need to know to speed things up.

If the person who needs to sign it off is going to be out of the office for two weeks, you need to find another way to get it done. You can't let these things drag on. It is in your interest to get this sorted out quickly.

Do whatever it takes. Don't just fill in the new hire acquisition form, fire it off to HR and forget it. That's what 99 out of 100 Hiring Managers do - they are so relieved that the whole thing is finished and believe their part in the process is over. But if the process is handled badly and the candidate decides not to take the job because of the delay then the candidate process will have to begin again.

Setting expectations is vital but try and exceed those expectations.

If you do set an expectation - that it will take two or three weeks before the written offer is sent - do what you can to beat that because it will give the candidate a really positive impression of you and the company.

Keeping in contact with the candidate is a crucial part of the process. Many organisations have really good procedures in place for maintaining contact with the new hire before they start. However, with key executives who often need to give notice periods of three months or more, contact can become sporadic and a bit impersonal.

Sending a brochure about the company in the post doesn't count as an effective 'contact'! And it's not enough to just invite the new hire to your next team-building or social event. You, the Hiring Manager, need to take responsibility for keeping in regular contact with your new hire. Draw up a proper communications plan.

Here's a sample LBA Communication Plan. (See page 92)

# LBA COMMUNICATIONS PLAN

| CANDIDATE UNDER OFFER: | Duncan Smith |
|---|---|
| START DATE: | 2nd October 2010 |
| **NEW EMPLOYEE COMMUNICATIONS PLAN** | |
| TELEPHONE CONTACT PLAN: | 1. Call scheduled every 2nd Friday for next 3 months at 8.30am to provide updates and discuss work challenges<br>2. No calls planned for August as Duncan away for 1st 2 weeks of August and Bob's holiday 2nd 2 weeks. |
| MEETING CONTACT PLAN: | 1. Duncan to attend the Sales Leadership Meeting on 2nd last Friday of the month (no call will take place on this day)<br>    a. Jenny to send out invites to Duncan<br>2. Bob to meet Duncan for dinner in the 2nd week in July to discuss output from the board meeting and reaction to half year results<br>    a. Jenny to organise<br>3. Duncan to attend Sales Managers' Away Day at end of September (2011 strategy and Budget Kick-Off)<br>    a. Jenny to send out invites to Duncan<br>4. Jenny to arrange Dinner with Eric Jones (Operations Director) & Harry Jeffs (Marketing Director) at back end of August<br>    a. Jenny to organise. |
| EVENTS PLAN: | 1. Jenny to send out invite to Duncan to Sales monthly team building event (usually a Thursday evening)<br>2. Jenny to send invite to Duncan for the Family Day to be held in July.<br>3. Jenny to send invite to Duncan to attend Brighton IPC Conference in September |
| COLLATERAL PLAN: | 1. Jenny to send Duncan press release for half year results announcement<br>2. Jenny to send new service delivery platform product launch collateral when available in August |
| COMMUNICATION PLAN DISTRIBUTION: | 1. Jenny Smith<br>2. Eric Jones<br>3. Harry Jeffs<br>4. Sales Management Team |
| HIRING MANAGER:<br><br>SIGNATURE: | **Bob Halliday** |

**LBA Communications Plan** – *Continuation Sheet (additional information)*

Yes, it may seem like hard work but having a written plan will help you keep on track. As with so many things if you write it down and take the time to plan it, you are much more likely to carry it out. It could be something like planning to speak every second Friday or sending them invitations to come into the office two or three times before they take up the new role.

Don't leave it to HR because it will be nowhere near as important to them as it is to you. It is all about taking ownership and saying "Right, this is important to me. I am going to make sure I get this person on board."

Schedule regular telephone calls and face to face meetings if possible with your new hire. Share information as much as you can. Obviously, some information will be confidential (until the candidate officially starts) but discuss the work to be done and the challenges ahead.

Of course your new hire will have their own workloads to manage so you will need to create the contact schedule with them.

Don't think you'll overwhelm the new candidate: I don't think I have ever known of anyone being put off because there has been too much contact from the new company.

Treat the recruit as far as you possibly can as if they have already started. You have invested a lot of effort in getting the person on board so don't mess it all up because you didn't manage the offer process properly.

This is a crucial period and you must manage it effectively.

## CHAPTER 11

# How To Start Off On The Right Foot

The final part of the process is the Performance Agreement which I touched upon earlier. This should be carried out as soon as possible – on the very first day the new hire starts if possible.

Remember, they've already had a chance to do some of the job in the interview process. They're ready to get stuck in.

This is the perfect time to revisit the outcomes you expect your new hire to achieve. Use the job specification you have created for this because it contains very specific objectives - performance and target measures - for your new hire to accomplish.

Of course, the objectives may have changed slightly and you may want to revisit some of those - maybe a different priority or a different objective has come up.

Go through the objectives again with your new hire, make it clear that is the target they need to aim to at least hit, if not surpass. From this discussion, create a Performance Agreement.

Will they balk at this kind of meeting during the first day on the job?

No way! High performing top drawer talent is not afraid of challenges. They don't look for ways to shirk their responsibilities. They really want to know what you expect from them and what you consider great performance to be.

And guess what? They'll be looking for ways to outperform against that. They'll want to do even better – they are high achievers by nature. It's what they've done throughout their careers and it's what they thrive on.

They will want to understand where the bar is so they can not only reach it but leap over it!

Here's a sample LBA Performance Agreement. (See page 97)

# LBA PERFORMANCE AGREEMENT

| ROLE: | SALES DIRECTOR - IT SERVICES |
|-------|------------------------------|

**PERFORMANCE AGREEMENT**

**Outcome 1 – Within 12 months, secure 5 new business deals with an order value of > £2M**

- Within 3 months, identify the top 10 new business prospects that have the potential to close in 2010 with an order value of greater than £2M
- Within 4 months, produce and implement a detailed opportunity activity plan to drive 5 x £2M+ opportunities to close by the end of 2010
- Within 6 months, qualify out deals with an order potential of less than £1M , which do not satisfy strategic deal criteria

**Outcome 2 – Within 12 months, secure 5 deals from strategic accounts with an order value > £3M**

- Within 2 months, review strategic account plans to support 'big deal' strategy
- Within 3 months, review strategic account team pipeline and identify top 10 accounts with £3M+ deal potential
- Within 4 months, produce and implement a detailed account management plans to drive 5 x £3M+ opportunities to close by the end of 2010
- Within 9 months, devise an ICT innovation seminar programme and sign-up 50 key execs from strategic accounts

**Outcome 3 – Improve sales team and account management performance by 30% (measured by achievement of target) within 12 months**

- Within 2 months, perform a sales and account team assessment review for all team members and identify skill gaps
- Within 3 months, prepare training development plans for each sales team and account team members to address skills gaps
- Within 4 months, present recommendations for sales team and account managers to UK Managing Director – no action, train, replace
- Within 12 months, improve opportunity conversion ratio to 30% from 19% by introducing stricter opportunity qualification and improving bid response quality
- Devise & Implement a new sales incentive scheme to drive individual and team sales performance within 3 months

## SIGNATURES

| Manager's Name: Bob Halliday | Name: Duncan Smith |
|------------------------------|--------------------|
| Role: Managing Director | Role: Sales Director |
| | |
| Signature: | Signature: |
| | |

**LBA PERFORMANCE AGREEMENT** – *Continuation Sheet (additional information)*

Why must you do this as soon as the new hire starts in the job? And what will happen if you don't have that initial agreement about the specific performance targets you expect the new hire to achieve?

Well, your new hire won't know what your expectations are. They may think they know but there will be a disparity between what they believe they should be doing and what you believe they should be doing. They won't know what you consider a great performance to be.

Many companies don't make the effort to set down in writing what they expect the new hires to achieve. Nothing is defined.

Once you have a Performance Agreement in place you have something to guide your meetings and discussions from day one. This is a really important part of the process. Remember your new hire has already had the opportunity to do some of the work in the job interview so it is not going to come as a bolt out of the blue – it's not going to be a big surprise to them. You'll have discussed the work to be done at some length during the offer management communication process so this won't be unexpected.

They will be prepped and ready to go; looking forward to getting stuck in.

So make sure you set some times aside to talk about the challenges ahead and the goals and objectives to be achieved and what success looks like. You need to make the objectives very specific and to have included them in the job specification so by this stage, it is something your new hire is completely familiar with.

Use the New Employee Performance Agreement template so you both have a record of it and both sign it. This will then become the foundation of future performance assessments.

Don't whatever you do make the mistake of leaving your new hire alone to 'find their feet'.

This 'sink or swim' attitude is ingrained in the culture of some companies, according to former Harvard Business School Professor and best-selling author Michael Watkins. He found that all too many companies believe that dropping a manager in at the deep end when they arrive is perceived to be a good yardstick as to whether they can cope with the job.

"During my research I did find 'sink or swim' cultures or leadership through Darwinian evolution. They throw people into the deep end and see what happens – if they sink they think they are better off without them. If they swim they must be great leaders, is the thinking. These days you cannot afford to have this precious talent flounder away."

This lack of training and communication in the first 90 days can spiral into a disaster for both the company and the individual. Within this period a manager will undoubtedly face a myriad of challenges that need to be tackled. This is a particularly hazardous period when alliances and first impressions are formed.

There are other things you need to do for your new hire to make sure that their first impressions of the company are favourable. The things that I'm about to recommend may seem obvious, even basic, but they are very important all the same. It's remarkable how often this stuff isn't done. I'm talking about things like making sure the new hire's laptop or PC and mobile phone are ready for them and that their email accounts work.

I've heard of people arriving at their new company only to discover that no one has organised a desk for them! Believe me, this happens. It is just another process that should be taken care of. As the Hiring Manager, you must make sure the process doesn't fall down for your new hire because it will give them a very poor impression about the company's attitude towards them.

I recommend that you create an introduction plan for your new hire so that they can meet their key colleagues, department heads, board members and whoever else they will need to meet.

Consider this to be part of the new hire's induction. Make sure that they meet the appropriate people at the appropriate times.

Not everyone is going to be there on day one, particularly if it is a national or international organisation. Take responsibility for organising introductions for your new hire.

They may have direct reports - they might be managing a team of line managers and they must meet or address them in some way. Allow time for the new hire to get their feet under the table and prepare their message before arranging such a meeting.

The employees who will be working for the new hire will form their own first impressions so to help ensure it's a positive impression, offer your new hire some guidance with an opening address.

This is one of those tasks that often gets overlooked or is not planned as well as it might be.

The induction process varies greatly from company to company - they range from a handshake and a coffee and a quick walk around the office with some smaller organisations to a full-blown, week-long series of meetings and presentations. Some global organisations get their new people to spend a week or two, sometimes longer, at the corporate headquarters.

The problem with induction programmes is that they tend to be one-size fits all. It is very difficult to pitch an induction programme at exactly the right level. Most induction programmes are designed for entry level staff because companies have a lot more entry level staff than executives. For that reason, be cautious about sending your new executive on a full-blown induction programme.

Executive hires require a tailored induction programme - some companies do this very well and some do it appallingly.

Making a distinction between the induction programme you offer to entry level staff and executive appointments is not elitist – it's about providing information that's appropriate.

Let's say you are the Hiring Manager in a five-star hotel – your induction programme for catering staff or chambermaids is likely to be very different to the induction programme you provide for departmental managers and senior executives.

**CHAPTER 12**

# How To Make Better Hiring Decisions

How can you ensure you hire the ideal candidate each time?

If you want to make better hiring decisions follow the *LBA Hiring Management System*™ which is proven to be more successful than the hit and miss approach many organisations take to making senior level hires.

The *LBA Hiring Management System*™ is a comprehensive eight phase system that encompasses the complete hiring process from beginning to end.

## Phase 1: Hiring Initiation Process

Clearly identify the business results you want and how you expect someone to achieve those results. This effectively answers the question of 'why' you are hiring someone and provides context to your search and breathes life into your hiring efforts.

Use the Hiring Initiation Document (HID) to elicit this information. As well as documenting the critical business results you need, it provides background and context. It also enables you to document a business case or ROI for your new hire, the people you anticipate being involved in the hiring process and their roles, plus a high-level plan with details of tasks and timescales.

To download a copy of your FREE Hiring Initiation Document (HID) please go to www.lauder-beaumont.com and click on the Download page.

## Phase 2: LBA Job Specification

To write an effective job specification, you need to think about outcomes and what will constitute success in the role.

Fast-forward 12 months and imagine that you are appraising the performance of the new hire. What would represent outstanding performance? This is invaluable for identifying the small number of performance indicators that will determine an individual's ultimate success or failure. Your job specification needs to be specific about the elements of the role which will determine success and the key challenges, problems and obstacles to be overcome in order to achieve success.

Success objectives must be linked to organisational or company objectives to be meaningful. They must flow down from the top. If you wind forward 12 months and think about what a successful outcome looks like, make sure you can map that onto an organisational or company goal.

If it doesn't contribute to achieving the higher level goals it will become a meaningless achievement 12 months on.

To download a copy of your FREE LBA Job Specification Template please go to www.lauder-beaumont.com and click on the Download page.

## Phase 3: LBA Sourcing Approach

The majority of sourcing strategies limit the size of the pool that you fish in. Unfortunately, very few top performers are swimming in shallow waters, hungry for your bait.

The top-performing talent is seldom proactively looking and almost never responds to job advertisements – they simply don't need to. They don't respond to amateur approaches from head-hunters either, politely passing on most opportunities presented.

Even when approached in a professional and intelligent manor, the majority will not respond positively but for a few, their interest may be stimulated if approached in the right way.

The LBA Sourcing approach delves into the depths where the top-performers reside. The approach to potential candidates is carefully crafted to attract high performers. There are no tricks and the approach isn't pushy or over-zealous. The approach is based on a deep understanding of the requirement and how to present it in a way to appeal to top-performers.

## Phase 4: Candidate Profiling

The over-reliance on CVs is a major contributor to making hiring mistakes. CVs come in all shapes and sizes and are extremely variable in terms of content. They are often full of ambiguous statements and irrelevant information.

Chances are the person you are looking for doesn't have a CV ready to go, off the shelf anyway. If they are happy in their current role, why would they?

Unfortunately, many, many great candidates are passed over simply because they don't have a CV ready to go and don't have either the time of inclination to produce one.

Forget CVs and start producing relevant and consistent candidate profiles in a format that will be useful when evaluating whether the person is a good match for the role and worth interviewing.

LBA Candidate Profiles run to a couple of pages at most and focus on the salient points which make a candidate relevant for the role.

They are produced by talking directly with the candidate using skilled questioning techniques that enables validation of the information and for it to be presented clearly and concisely without the 'gloss' that is contained in a typical CV.

To download a copy of your FREE LBA Candidate Profile template please go to www.lauder-beaumont.com and click on the Download page.

## Phase 5: LBA Interview Approach

The problem with almost all interviews is that they are purely question and answer based and focussed on past performance, i.e. what candidates have done (or claim they have done) rather than what they can do.

Behavioural interviews for example look at how candidates reacted to a situation in the past to predict future behaviour.

What these interviews don't do is give the candidate an opportunity to prove that they can do the specific job that you have on offer today right there and then in the interview - but they should.

The *LBA Hiring Management System*™ provides a framework for designing an interview to get the candidate either doing the job or at least parts of the job in the interview; tackling real problems that they will be responsible for should they secure the role.

The interviewer is encouraged to use the meeting as a working session with a colleague, rather than treat it as an interview. Other team members and colleagues may be invited to join the working session to assess how they interact.

With the LBA interview approach, there are no clever and perfect answers to questions – doing the job leaves nowhere to hide. The expert, high performing candidates don't look for hiding places, they can't wait to show you what they can do!

## Phase 6: Post Interview Evaluation

This now becomes a simple task. You have seen the potential candidates in action and it will now be obvious who the outstanding candidate for the job is.

If it isn't, the hiring system has broken down somewhere or you haven't seen the right person.

In attempt to stop Hiring Managers making decisions based on first impressions or gut feel, organisations have introduced complex evaluation systems, often involving some sort of grading or scoring system.

If you've conducted the correct type of interview (that is, to get the candidate to perform the job with you in the interview) these systems are not necessary. They are just more numbers to hide behind when the hire doesn't work out!

## Phase 7: Offer Management

You've identified the person you want to hire; the next step is to negotiate and hopefully agree an offer acceptable to both parties. The parameters of the offer should have been discussed early in the process, usually in the initial conversation with the candidate so there should be no big surprises. The offer negotiation shouldn't be overly drawn out but do expect to negotiate.

Once a verbal offer is agreed, the written paperwork must follow as soon as possible. Understanding your internal process and anticipated timescales is vital, as is accurately communicating this to your new employee. The Hiring Manager should take the lead here and should ride the internal process as hard as possible to ensure that expectations are met.

Many organisations have good intentions and procedures in place to keep in regular contact with the new hire before they start.

With top-performing talent, notice periods are often three months plus. Despite best intentions, communication with the new recruit is often sporadic and impersonal. The Hiring Manager should take ownership here and draw up a communications plan. It's not enough to send a few brochures and ask your new employee to your next team social event. Regular telephone calls and face-to-face meetings should be scheduled as appropriate. Share as much information as you can, discuss the work to be done, discuss any new thoughts that you have about the challenges ahead; in other words , treat the new recruit as far as possible as if they had already started.

The *LBA Hiring Management System*™ provides communications templates so that you can plan your new hire interactions before they start.

To download a copy of your FREE LBA Communications template, please go to www.lauder-beaumont.com and click on the Download page.

## Phase 8: Performance Agreement

This should be drawn up as soon as possible when your new employee starts – the very first day if you can.

Remember that your new hire has already had an opportunity to do some or all of the job in the interview and you will have continued to discuss the work to be done at some length during the offer management communication process.

The new hire will be charged up and ready to go.

Before they get stuck in, take some time to set out the challenges ahead, the goals and objectives to be achieved and what success looks like. Make the objectives very specific and make sure they are measurable.

There should be no surprises because they should closely mirror the items listed in the job specification.

Agree what acceptable and outstanding performance looks like and sign up to it.

The *LBA Hiring Management System*™ includes a New Employee Performance Agreement template to capture and record this agreement.

To obtain your FREE New Employee Performance Agreement template please go to www.lauder-beaumont.com and click on the Download page.

## TESTIMONIALS

# What Clients Say About Lauder Beaumont

"Since I met Rob and he introduced me to the *LBA Hiring Management System*, it has transformed the way I approach hiring and has dramatically improved my success rate. The new sales executives I hired as a result of working with Rob and using the *LBA Hiring Management System* are still with me 2 years on and delivering results.

"Lauder Beaumont Associates provide more than just a professional headhunting service. I choose to rely on their knowledge and experience to reduce the time taken when searching for new members of staff and more importantly, I know that when they introduce a candidate, they have already been through the first interview stage!

"When I was asked to rebuild the new business sales team, I decided I needed to work with a specialist organisation, themselves made up of professionals who I would want working for me. Such an attribute, in my experience, is a definite unique selling point. Lauder Beaumont Associates understand the issues I face because they have actually fulfilled similar roles themselves. This understanding has directly led to my new team achieving early success and moving on to hitting their annual targets.

"Finally, there is a cost associated with recruitment; false economy and short-cuts may reduce initial outgoings however when the new joiner success rate is paired with business achieved, there is no doubt Lauder Beaumont Associates and the *LBA Hiring Management System* are in a league of one. I would not hesitate to recommend them."

*Brady K. Davis, New Business Sales Manager,*
*SunGard Availability Services (UK) Limited*

"As the VP of HR & Learning outsourcing in EMEA I have used Lauder Beaumont Associates to help me find some of the key roles I need to ensure that we deliver the right solutions for our clients. Rob and the team at Lauder Beaumont Associates have been excellent at finding the "hard to get skills" that we need. As compared to other agencies that I work with Lauder Beaumont Associates has...

- listened well to our specifications

- found a good slate of candidates, even for the toughest challenges

- worked as a team with IBM to make sure the candidate understands the role and the team they will be coming into

- managed communications well on all sides

- taken time to really understand the IBM team, organisation and structure, so they can position the role correctly the first time to potential candidates

And more important we have gotten results and the Lauder Beaumont Associates team are easy to work with."

*Mary Sue Rogers,*
*VP of HR and Learning Outsourcing for IBM EMEA*


"I was trying to hire Senior Data Centre Sales Consultants against a very tight brief, which made these individuals extremely difficult to find and attract. A key part of the brief was that I needed candidates based in mainland Europe rather than the UK to service client demand in this region. Sun had previously enlisted the services of a well known headhunting brand to source candidates with limited success. Working with Rob at Lauder Beaumont Associates was a different experience and I could tell that Rob really understood the brief as a result of taking the time to actually listen to what I needed. Rob identified a suitable and interested candidate within a matter of days who was ideally located in the Netherlands – something that was previously not accomplished. If you are looking to employ difficult to obtain talent in the UK or Europe, I would have no hesitation in recommending Rob."

*Grant Cooper, Sun Microsystems,*
*Head of Data Centre Efficiency EMEA and APAC*

"I had been looking for a Sales Director for our industrial coatings business, for some months, with no success. On a personal recommendation, I met with Rob from Lauder Beaumont Associates.

Despite operating in a completely new market sector, Rob was able to successfully find suitable candidates, from whom I chose my Sales Director. More than this, I was most impressed with how Rob conducted himself throughout the process. The key points that made Lauder Beaumont Associates stand out for me were:

- The careful attention paid to selecting candidates who properly fitted the brief provided

- The excellent communication and management of expectations

- The honesty

Not only do I recommend Lauder Beaumont Associates to people that I know, I have recommended to Rob that he should consider looking at market segments that he has not previously considered."

*Jonathan Robson, Managing Director,*
*Becker Acroma Limited*


"We have an excellent history of working with Rob Andrews to find senior BPO leaders across Europe. Rob is quickly able to understand our challenges and our business environment, and this in turn means that he is a very efficient and effective head hunter to work with. I also find Rob very good at developing relationships with the candidates, and maintaining these relationships throughout the recruitment process. Thirdly, Rob is very good in the advice he gives me on what the candidate is thinking, and on how to close the deals."

*Chris Sutton, Managing Director,*
*Global Business Process Outsourcing, Logica*

# SPECIAL LIMITED OFFER FOR READERS OF THIS BOOK

## *Here's How To Hire Top Performing Talent*

# A FREE LBA HIRING MANAGEMENT SYSTEM CONSULTATION WORTH £1,500

I am offering a FREE face to face 1½ hour consultation to help you use the hugely successful *LBA Hiring Management System* for your next hire.

This is a completely free 1½ hour consultation with me, Rob Andrews, the author of this book and creator of the *LBA Hiring Management System*.

It is an exclusive offer for readers of this book – you must quote this reference **LBABO50** to book your consultation.

This offer is strictly limited to 50 consultations. Personal consultations are normally charged at £1,000 per hour – so sign up now for your free consultation and £1,500 saving!

To qualify for this one-off, free 1½ hour consultation, you must be a hiring manager or an HR executive with direct hiring responsibility.

### ONLY 50 SLOTS AVAILABLE IN 2010

Free consultations are offered on a first come first served basis, so take action now. The only way to book your free 1½ hour consultation is to register your details now – at:

### **www.lauder-beaumont.com/free-consultation.html**
and quote this reference number **LBABO50** (UK only)

I look forward to hearing from you!

*Rob Andrews*

**Rob Andrews**
*Lauder Beaumont Associates (LBA)*